Awakening from Dawn to Dusk

A Perspective Shift Into Greater Freedom

Ron Baron

Awakening from Dawn to Dusk

A Perspective Shift
Into Greater Freedom

Ron Baron

SPOTLIGHT
PUBLISHING HOUSE
Goodyear, Arizona

Introduction

How to approach and read this book:

This book is derived from a greater understanding that originated from an out-of-body experience. The hope is to bring a unique twist into view, have it be entertaining, and place an eye-opening spin on reality. Other content has been carefully reworded to help stimulate and inspire you to consider stepping out of your comfort zone.

Having a near-death experience (NDE) helped to *reset* my mind and body, and it soon became apparent that despite the absolute truth existing everywhere, our mind instantly removes it from view and, for purposes of understanding and finding ways to relate to it, creates a reality around it. The concept of 'absolute truth' was thought up to imply one way and one way only. In this book, we consider it to mean the 'is-ness' of things (the literal, energetic, cellular vibrations intrinsic in all things that exist before we even give them a name). Using limited language, our self-centered mind then superimposes interpretations to relate with one another.

Gaining value from this book will require your willingness to be objective and the ability to step away from how you currently hold the *absolute truth* and acknowledge the truths that you now embrace are all relative truths, also known as reality. Reality is the only thing that exists inside a human mind and is what we use to navigate life.

Daily thoughts to ponder will reappear and be woven with a common thread. Repetition has always proven to be our best form of learning.

You may find that some passages are more profound than others and ignite a spark inside of you. Feel free to extract them to keep them responsibly in your awareness throughout your day. You may also use the camera on your cell phone to capture inspiring words. Feel free to share them with others to keep them alive and incorporate them.

Many of the paragraphs have been purposefully written in the first person for greater intimacy and a sense of oneness. Feel free to take any passage that moves or touches you and make it your own. The more inspired you are to share your new perspectives, the more you acknowledge this book as a gift.

Consider these small passages to be special moments in our time together, one for each day of the year. (you get your money's worth on leap year – lol)

Each morning, upon waking, and every evening before bedtime, you can take the time to embrace a new point of view and allow it to sink in.

Some thoughts are simple and to the point, while others require deeper contemplation.

Let them fill your heart and mind with inspiration, hope, and promise for greater moments of freedom.

Carpe Diem with Joy and Wonder.

A Thought to Ponder at Dawn

Blessed am I who is, no matter what, capable of seeing the authentic beauty in things.

Blessed am I when I consciously create my reality inside a world of illusion, for I can embrace unbridled freedom and joy.

"Reality is an illusion, albeit a persistent one."

Thank you, Dr. Albert Einstein, for helping me to understand this.

A Thought to Ponder at Dusk

My reality and identity constitute my entire "B"elief "S"ystem, which yields the infamous acronym *BS*.

I will come to recognize that my BS is both healthy and unhealthy depending on what I'm thinking because they are all part of my Belief System.

My *BS* is all that I have because no *TS*, "T"ruth "S"ystem has yet to exist. Knowing this allows me access to recreate a new reality as I watch unhealthy beliefs neutralize.

This is a powerful perspective and portal to my spiritual émancipation.

A Thought to Ponder at Dawn

The thought process that gives rise to my current belief system is not the same one that will allow my mind to transform and expand.

At any point, I can tap into infinite consciousness and gain a greater perspective, first by asking a specific question, then by quieting myself down in stillness, and then being focused on listening with enthusiasm.

I will learn over time to trust the information that comes to mind, especially when I'm clear that I'm not thinking, only listening.

A Thought to Ponder at Dusk

Who I am in the world is a reflection of who you, I, and others, say that I am.

Although validated in part by collective opinion, I remain aware of life's constant flux and can choose to redefine myself at will.

My attachment to popular consensus can generate some lessons around self-worth, freedom, inner joy, and happiness.

A Thought to Ponder at Dawn

When my center of focus is in the *now*, time and space disappear.

The shift that occurs goes from *Chronos* time, which is found on ticking clocks, to *Kairos* time, which is where the sense of time disappears, leaving us in the now.

When I'm fascinated by someone or something and lose track of time and space, Kairos time makes Chronos time pass by quite rapidly.

It is in the *now* moments where passion, inspiration, and authentic love connect my heart and mind.

A Thought to Ponder at Dusk

In a community setting, my mind searches hard to figure out where it best fits in.

When blind to universal *oneness*, my mind conjures up that it is separate from others and does everything it can to belong, oftentimes to the point of sheer exhaustion.

The irony is that on a cosmic scale, we are all made up of stardust, which makes me connected to everything no matter what my mind might decide to invent.

A Thought to Ponder at Dawn

If both Nothing and Everything is thought to be *true*, then I can only have a *belief* about the existence of absolute truth because the word 'absolute', implies one way, and one way only.

Too often, the relative truth is used interchangeably with the absolute truth. This is a huge mistake and gets confusing at times because it short circuits my thinking process.

I, therefore, surrender the idea that the *absolute* truth doesn't exist, the relative truth is nothing more than what I believe in my own (relative) reality, and that I can alter my reality any time I choose by tapping into an infinite realm of realities.

A Thought to Ponder at Dusk

The usage of the words, *I*, *me*, and *my*, is a reason why we even have conversations about *oneness*.

Without adding the *self* into a conversation, the need to distinguish *oneness* disappears.

The irony is that the reality in which we all agree to live requires its verbiage to distinguish our physical separateness from everyone.

A way for me to get through this illusory life challenge is to remember that "I am unique, just like *everyone* else."

A Thought to Ponder at Dawn

When I tap into a greater consciousness, I have a shift in perspective that allows me to create new interpretations which are more in line with being in service to humanity.

The act of being in any kind of purposeful service blankets me with a sense of power, accomplishment, and gratitude.

A Thought to Ponder at Dusk

Self-Realization is present when I am fully engaged and relating to others while simultaneously being detached from all outcomes.

Add to that a heightened sense of clarity and indifference, causing all positive and negative interpretations to neutralize themselves.

This tends to engulf the mind and body with an energetic sense of heaven on earth.

A Thought to Ponder at Dawn

Fear and uncertainty are part of everyone's human experience.

When my fear and uncertainty shift into authentic love and trust for the greater good and order in things, I come closer to understanding what self-realization requires.

Forging my path to enlightenment is not about reaching a destination, it's about embracing an incredible way of being.

A Thought to Ponder at Dusk

Being on a continual journey to enlightenment is as much of an illusion as always being at the starting point of every moment.

The major difference is that one illusion simply keeps the freshness alive.

Recalling that realities are all made up helps remind me of the importance to choose wisely.

The key for me is to believe that what I create is possible and then live into it with all of my heart and soul as if the quality of my life depends on it because it does.

A Thought to Ponder at Dawn

Knowing about being in the moment and being in the moment are two separate things. When my mind is focused and centered at the moment, it is unaware of the thought of being in it.

Being in a moment comes and goes so quickly at times, unless I'm in deep meditation; the instant that my mind thinks about the moment that it's in, it's no longer in it because it just became history.

Being present in the preciousness of moments is as beautiful as being in a deep meditative state, where anything is possible and all is well, always. I am also here to enjoy my human experience where my focus is to relate with other people's realities, which is completely a horse of a different color. I realize the importance of balancing those two vantage points.

A Thought to Ponder at Dusk

Things that have mattered in the past usually continue to impact the current state of affairs and are also a good indication of what to expect in a probable future.

Access to sustaining freedom from my past is to reevaluate all my beliefs as being only beliefs and not truths.

This is especially for the dysfunctional ones as they too are all illusions. The repetitive practice of implementing new perspectives in their place will eventually serve me better.

A Thought to Ponder at Dawn

One perspective of enlightenment is having a mindset that is sustainably awakened and consciously clear while knowing that human reality is nothing more than an illusion.

An enlightened mind accepts and allows everyone and everything to exist as it does without looking to change or alter it; this is also called conditional love.

The walk of an enlightened being is to be intentionally focused as an observer and fully engaged as a journeyman through life.

A Thought to Ponder at Dusk

Each mind comes with its own identity and ego, which was inherited from past generations.

All beliefs are then perpetuated by my mind's *buy-in* to whatever it was taught.

An *awakened* mind has been emancipated from the entanglement which was once governed by its own rules and regulations.

A Thought to Ponder at Dawn

The inherited community, culture, and environment in which I was born and lived as a child, have formed most of my current beliefs and reality.

Both healthy and unhealthy beliefs remain to this day.

By choosing a community of like-minded people who possess the kind of beliefs that I aspire to, I can learn and eventually self-generate a more appealing quality of beliefs that will directly impact my life in a great way.

Transforming my life into something more worthwhile and resulting from my own design will come by incorporating healthier and more satisfying beliefs repeatedly and with discipline.

A Thought to Ponder at Dusk

Not only do I see the world through spectacles of beliefs that I've inherited from previous generations, but I also reinforce these interpretations and then use them as my telescope to perpetually see the world as I do. This limits my ability to imagine outside my box without prejudice and I tend to default to what is safe and familiar.

Although my interpretations are subjective and limited, self-reflection is like a new set of eyes that lets me look at my operating system with greater clarity and understanding. I have every opportunity to access a new and expanding reality when the one I have is obsolete.

A Thought to Ponder at Dawn

Our mind believes that the world we see outside gives us our reality, when in fact our mind's reality is what gives us the world that we see outside.

Just like the illusion of the sun rising and setting, when it never moves at all, I live inside of the illusion that there is actually an *out there*, when in fact every ounce of meaning and understanding has been generated inside of my mind.

A Thought to Ponder at Dusk

The world outside *is* the mirror that reflects my mind's belief system and shifts only when my inner world transforms.

I am open to contemplating that everything about me and the world around me, is made up and based on individual and collective agreement.

Day 11

A Thought to Ponder at Dawn

An enlightened being lives in a sustainable awakened state of infinite connection and neutrality.

This is also called Christ Consciousness or Self-Realization and is uncommon and rarely seen, although possible.

Those who possess this magnificent form of mindfulness tend to remain very modest, are unassuming, non-reactive, and approach all of life with kindness and love.

A Thought to Ponder at Dusk

When we realize that an experience *is* an experience itself, it is *true* as it is, without any wiggle room for it to be any other way.

Everyone's mind, however, instantly responds by interpreting *every* experience as quickly as possible and in doing so, removes the *truth* from it and places the 'isness' of it into the realm of reality.

Said differently, the process of interpreting an experience voids the *truth* and creates the illusion of *reality* where everyone's interpretations are valid and meaningful.

A Thought to Ponder at Dawn

To create the illusion of getting from *here to there*, we must perpetuate thoughts of an imaginary future that is expressed in the present moment.

Never mind that in *truth*, there isn't any 'there' to get to, while in reality there most certainly is.

I live inside of an illusion that is given by time and space, while no other species lives by these rules and as a result, remains free.

A Thought to Ponder at Dusk

When we stand 'in-lightenment', we *are* in sync with consciousness itself.

This occurs rarely and is an incredible gift given to the human mind.

What this boils down to is the ability to tap into creation itself.

Being aware that I am consciousness itself, remains my access to all that is possible.

Day 13

A Thought to Ponder at Dawn

Whenever my mind is upset, it is living inside of past thoughts. When it is anxious, it dances with thoughts of a future.

The moment that I take a break and clear my mind of thought, even for only a short period, there is a remarkable sense of peace and calm which allows my center of power to return.

A Thought to Ponder at Dusk

Should a man choose to look down upon another, let it be only to extend a helping hand.

Anyone who says that they don't judge others is either fooling themselves, not human, or fully enlightened because it is part of our human design to assess, evaluate and judge things.

Assisting anyone who needs help is not only self-gratifying, it helps the flow of life to cycle smoothly.

A Thought to Ponder at Dawn

All forms of communication, language being one of them, are how we create collective agreements to keep our realities alive.

Being mindful of the limitations which are inherent in all forms of communication, makes it easier to be modest and compassionate to our own communication skills.

If we didn't have access to this limited way of relating to people, places, and things, we'd not have a way to relate to a human experience.

A Thought to Ponder at Dusk

Being literally *out of one's mind*, sometimes allows one's reality to reset itself and fosters the impetus to generate and support a new reality with a new language.

Having a near-death experience is one way while having life-threatening challenges is another opportunity for this to occur.

A much easier and more pleasant way in which to expand consciousness, however, is through deep traditional meditation where the mind finds itself empty of thought.

With repetition, what develops is a new realm of thinking and freedom. Now is my opportunity to choose meditation as an effective practice and reinforcement that will allow a greater quality of life

Day 15

A Thought to Ponder at Dawn

Creating a new language is a great way in which to accommodate an always-expanding consciousness.

This task requires both creating new words along with newly associated meanings, and also giving new meanings to already existing words.

A new language will gain a strong foundation of strength once there is enrollment and collective agreement. Language has been reworked and recreated since the beginning of mankind, no sense stopping now.

A Thought to Ponder at Dusk

Throughout the years, my reality has illustrated that I'm pretty much always right about my take on things, even on the occasions when I'm wrong, I'm right about that too!

If I'm right most of the time, how then is it possible for everyone to also be right? Every mind craves understanding and creates whatever it believes to be right.

When done without mindfulness, it is the cause of war, and hatred, and is disrespectful of our differences.

Therefore, it is important to choose being kind over right when the option is available.

Day 16

A Thought to Ponder at Dawn

Throughout my life, I have never felt myself to be radiantly beautiful or handsome.

One day I came upon the magnificent beauty of my own spirit's reflection.

Now I'm able to see yours.

I will remind people of their own illumination and brilliance.

A Thought to Ponder at Dusk

A cause-and-effect relationship is intrinsic to understanding the natural order of things.

Chances are there is a limitless number of cosmic laws yet to be realized when it comes to understanding creation itself.

Realizing that a miracle is nothing more than an unknown cosmic law helps to remove the mysticism and fantasy from the word *miracle.*

A Thought to Ponder at Dawn

The complexity of the human mind distinguishes us from all other species of animals.

Even within my species, the many levels of consciousness are a result of the various levels of focus and free will. The time is now to be more compassionate and forgiving to everyone for being exactly where they are in their lives, including me.

Nothing ever stays the same, which can be a saving grace when personal growth and development are concerned.

An enlightened mind knows that the *outside* world is generated inside of itself and loses the perspective of blaming or judging any outside circumstances.

A Thought to Ponder at Dusk

Simply put, creating language requires making up words, attaching meaning to them, and then incorporating collective agreement to make it all real, significant and *meaningful*.

Speaking something *generatively* into reality is an inspiration for what is new and not a fix for what is old. Trying to speak something completely generative which has never been spoken before by anyone is one of my life's greatest challenges.

A Thought to Ponder at Dawn

There isn't a University of Advanced Knowledge on earth where you can be awarded a degree in Spiritual, Energetic, or Universal Wisdom. Wisdom comes from with 'in', while knowledge often comes from the outside or from with 'out'.

Knowledge is to the mind, as wisdom is to the soul.

Ironically, wisdom becomes available usually after life's challenges of pain or suffering heal.

The question becomes whether or not I'm willing to embrace that opportunity.

A Thought to Ponder at Dusk

As a collective global network of consciousness, we continue to agree and believe that who we are is generated from our thoughts about who we are, as well as the thoughts which others believe about us.

This can't be any further from the *truth*, but it's what we've got to go with. Who I am is who I say I am and what is needed as a result is for me to behave in a manner consistent with my word.

Honoring my words as a direct reflection of myself is foundational to having integrity.

Day 19

A Thought to Ponder at Dawn

Having any sense of a *starting point* fosters the illusion that there is someplace to get to.

Learning that there is something called, 'over there, is what makes it possible to go from point A to point B.

Spiritualists tell us that there is only the here and now and no place to get to. This is an example of how multiple realities can not only exist at the same time but also yield different behaviors and actions taken.

It reinforces the importance of connecting with others who have similar realities to have some sense of comfort while respecting those who don't.

A Thought to Ponder at Dusk

Attempts to control my mind's thoughts are challenging and oftentimes unsuccessful.

To illustrate this point, I'll set a timer for one minute, close my eyes, and try to think of absolutely nothing for only 60 seconds - without devoted practice, it's almost impossible!

Being awake to the actual thought process which occurs, followed by allowing and accepting it to be as it is, helps to expand self-awareness and allows my light as the *witnessing observer* to shine bright.

A Thought to Ponder at Dawn

Being *awake* means that I've accessed a perspective that is outside the realm of normal thinking, realizing that I am the consciousness that is housed inside of a human earth suit and experience.

When the *spirit* that *I am* takes the front row center seat in the auditorium of my mind, I can watch my body and mind put on an amazing live performance.

Shifting into this vantage point for only minutes each day can expand my reality.

A Thought to Ponder at Dusk

Permitting myself to powerfully surrender to *the flow* of life itself can profoundly reset the quality of my daily life, the person I am, and take way less effort.

A Thought to Ponder at Dawn

In addition to life and death both being illusions, my entire identity and reality are both made up as well.

Realize and sustaining this perspective daily, will certainly shift my energy on a cellular level as well as alter my physiology in a great way.

This increases the probability of enjoying a lifetime of sustainable freedom and happiness to be within reach.

A Thought to Ponder at Dusk

The art of failing is a powerful tool when distinguished as being separate from one's identity or self-worth.

Failure allows what's missing to reveal itself and for correction and advancement to be made.

Although my past relationship with failure may not have been completely healthy, I now choose my failures as a powerfully transformative tool for growth and development.

A Thought to Ponder at Dawn

My mind creates fear from a perception of uncertainty which in turn, produces a spontaneous reaction causing me to return to a comforting sense of safety and security.

The irony is that both the stimulus (fear), and the response (reactive behavior, usually fight or flight), are illusions that were made up inside of my mind, to begin with.

Being in action in the face of fear is called courage. Taking action helps fears to transform and disappear in their own time.

A Thought to Ponder at Dusk

Being a sourcing assistant for others to self-generate their own greatness is a core sentiment of every enlightened individual.

Much like many other species, humankind is wired to depend on fellowship and community to thrive and sustain itself. Although bad apples may tend to destabilize the bunch, the heartbeat sentiments of the herd's majority are what determine their probability and predictability of survival.

This doesn't mean that good always triumphs over evil; what ends up thriving is a direct function of what has been fueled and reinforced.

A Thought to Ponder at Dawn

The key to enjoying an enlightened life is having a committed practice of remaining awake and aware of both my body's physicality and my mind's thought processes.

Just as I have my daily habitual routines, so too is my practice of remaining conscious.

Whether I begin by setting a cell phone timer every two hours to remind me to stop and take a moment to think of something different that I'm grateful for or making sure that I stop for a short pause to breathe in peace and calm, I will implement these sacred mini- breaks into my daily life.

A Thought to Ponder at Dusk

Making a living is creating a quality of life that is consistent with the belief that I have about myself.

Making money, however, is what supports the quality of living that I've chosen.

A Thought to Ponder at Dawn

Nature has designed life and death to be in a state of continuous flow.

To master the streaming of life itself with a sense of fun, ease, and deep satisfaction, it is wise to give up swimming against the current of the inevitable and hop on the inner tube.

There's so much more richness and meaning added when I *go with the flow*.

A Thought to Ponder at Dusk

Who I am is a direct result of the quality of all my inner thoughts and communications.

Aware of it or not, the outcome, whatever it might be, doesn't just happen by accident, it is a habitual lifestyle practice.

Being awake, responsible, and accountable for my thoughts and communications, is one of the most priceless gifts I give to myself.

A Thought to Ponder at Dawn

A Formula for Creation:
Idea + Focused Intention + Action = Manifestation.

This is synonymous with: Inspiration + Intelligence + Movement = Result.

Although all words are key, action and movement are critical for why manifestation and results might not occur.

A Thought to Ponder at Dusk

Being present and thoughtless simultaneously is usually achieved in meditation and places me in a state of *truthfulness*.

Also known as the *isness* of someone or something, the *truth* can only be embraced in a realm of awakened mindlessness.

The moment my mind begins to think, reality sets in, and the *truth* is gone!

A Thought to Ponder at Dawn

No matter how open-minded or *out of the box* I believe that I can think, I can only come from a single mind's perspective of what the box's boundaries are.

My mind's capacity to simultaneously have multiple perspectives is possible, but certainly not easy - it takes discipline, focus, and lifestyle practice.

A Thought to Ponder at Dusk

Gandhi was right when he said, *"Be the change that you wish to see"*, and here's why...

Only I can envision and be that which I wish to see in the world because I *am* the source of the world that I see.

The world that I see is all generated inside of my mind.

A Thought to Ponder at Dawn

People have the same experience when they are together watching something. My personal interpretation of an experience, however, is what may cause me to react differently.

Experiences are different from interpretations; experiences are pure while interpretations are specific to an individual's point of view.

My current interpretations are almost always based on both my past interpretations and the knowledge which I've acquired.

Realizing this allows me to be solely responsible for my interpretations which create my reality.

A Thought to Ponder at Dusk

When I've been asked, "Who am I being?" or "Who am I?", *being* (used as a noun), is unable to answer that question.

There is not yet a language that exists for the *being* that lives inside of my body. Instead, those questions require my *knowledge* to create an interpretation of what a *being* is.

Knowing is the processing and assimilation of data that exists inside of my mind. A *being* is who *I am* - it's pure and exists *as it is* and for always.

A Thought to Ponder at Dawn

Without a mind, there are simply no thoughts or any awareness of awareness itself, and lastly, no reality as well.

Without exception, my mind creates everything that I think and believe by translating thought energy into thoughts. Consciousness itself, which is what *I am*, and a part of, simply *is*.

In a human experience, I can embrace it all. When my mind is on, I am present with my thoughts and have my reality to contend with. When my mind is quiet, I have the opportunity to be *me*, an individual expression of awareness.

A Thought to Ponder at Dusk

My mind is sometimes awake yet most times asleep.

Aware of it or not, it always runs the show, giving meaning to everything it sees and does.

When it acknowledges *my presence*, it illuminates my mind into a clearer and more blissful state until sooner or later, it falls back to sleep.

A lifetime practice to remain awakened by using meditation is a great gift for me.

Day 29

A Thought to Ponder at Dawn

My eyes see the beautiful *spirit* in others when whatever is blinding them is cleared away.

I alone am responsible for having a clear vision.

The quality of my vision determines the integrity of my connection to everyone and everything.

A Thought to Ponder at Dusk

The state of enlightenment remains in existence when it is a lifetime and lifestyle practice.

My practice includes having my mind remain awake to who *I am* - the spirit temporarily residing within a human 'earth suit' - as well as being mindful of every spirit that inhabits other human bodies.

Holding this in reverence allows me to embrace my amazing mortal life in a new way.

A Thought to Ponder at Dawn

When my mind realizes that who *I am* is the *spirit* inside, it bows to me in gratitude and service and awakens me to a more mindful life.

Realizing that which *I am, you are,* opens my conscious connection to a boundless network of energy.

Hosting this expanded awareness, confirms and helps me to access infinite possibilities.

A Thought to Ponder at Dusk

Language is a beautiful, yet limited method of how we all communicate. I assimilate collectively agreed-upon words and concepts to give a voice to the perspective that I created regarding my experiences.

Some amazing perceptions have no words because they are simply unavailable in language. For example, should I try to put words into a Biography about God, it could never provide appropriate justice.

Ironically, it's comforting to realize that the things that words cannot accurately or precisely describe, remain present in my heart and mind.

A Thought to Ponder at Dawn

Our life existence doesn't mean anything until both you and I fill it up with meaning. Life is simply life — it begins as a white canvas and then receives brush strokes of various colors throughout the years.

The wiser I become, the more attention I pay to the brushes and paints that I choose to work with to create my masterpiece. Living my life to create passion and purpose is synonymous with living a life of joy and abundance.

A Thought to Ponder at Dusk

Acknowledging the *I am* that *I am*, is fine although most often meaningless and noncontributory when dealing with my daily existence.

The "I, me, and my," which are part of my mind's ego, are the reasons why there is even a need for conversations about *oneness*. Without the illusion of having a *self-involved* conversation, oneness disappears.

One main reason for having a human experience is so that the self can learn to be expressed.

The huge blunder that occurs is not realizing or acknowledging that the expressions of other-selves are just as valid and deserving of mutual respect and admiration.

A Thought to Ponder at Dawn

Realizing that *I am* neither my mind nor body, the question becomes, "Who then am I?"

The answer?

I am the illumination that allows my mind the clarity to even ask that question. *I am* is a *light* of awareness, an *observer*, and nothing more.

My light helps my mind to see things more clearly.

A Thought to Ponder at Dusk

Many of us are born, live a fairly decent life, and then die without ever having had a play with our greater consciousness.

Some might agree that they are lucky for having missed out on the uncomfortable challenges that conscious awakening sometimes bestows on the psyche.

Awareness is consciousness turning the lights on and allowing the mind to see itself with greater clarity — for some, it is blinding, while for others, it is emancipating.

A Thought to Ponder at Dawn

There is never any tension between deep beliefs and my actions.

Unease begins to occur when my mind gains another perspective that has the potential to make my current beliefs obsolete. Tension increases because my mind's ego is confronted with something new and unknown, causing a serious threat of potentially having to give up familiar beliefs.

The mind's drama can be a rollercoaster ride especially when it hasn't learned to be more stable and accepting of life's temporality. Where in my day ahead might I anticipate feeling tension and be mindful of flexibility?

A Thought to Ponder at Dusk

A breakdown becomes a breakthrough when I powerfully surrender and release the strong hold on my current vantage point in consideration of incorporating a new one.

Although this is easier said than done, it works like a charm.

A Thought to Ponder at Dawn

Who I am is what I pretend to be.

Who others are, I pretend them to be the way I say they are as well.
I may feel and say that I am a certain way, but that's also made up too.
When I fully embrace my life both as real and pretend, as all of the
characters at Disney are, I've then mastered my life on earth

A Thought to Ponder at Dusk

A happy life is sustainable when there's a harmonious balance between
what I'm attempting to create in my day and how the day turns out.

Plus, should the day not turn out as planned, my inner peace and
calm are my salvation.

I breathe in peace, calm, and joy into every breath before I drift off
into sleep.

A Thought to Ponder at Dawn

Being mindful of the illusory outside world and knowing that everyone and everything is a carbon copy of what exists inside of my mind, is a continual confirmation that I've been the creator all along.

Embracing and owning my power allows me access to freedom and joy beyond words.

A Thought to Ponder at Dusk

In retrospect, the onset of my identity was a funny gag gift inherited from dead people.

Everyone who came before me contributed to the identity I'm so familiar with.

I then perpetuated it because that was all I knew how to do.

I wonder what my life would look like now if I was aware of this from the start.

I seriously consider what my life will look like now that I have the complete say in how things will go for me from this moment on.

A Thought to Ponder at Dawn

A self-realized person engages and remains detached from their identity and the world around them, gifting them with a perspective of heaven on earth.

My resistance to detaching from my identity stands in the way of unbridled freedom and joy, and the quality of my life depends upon it.

The Ultimate Failure is to ever think that who I am is my identity because it keeps me in a world of limitation.

When I realize that I can *have* an identity instead of allowing my identity to *have* me, I gain access to *all that is possible*.

A Thought to Ponder at Dusk

My reality is the collective interpreted experiences that are neither fixed nor true, yet I hold onto many of these beliefs as if they were.

When consciousness expands, I'm able to see the temporality and absence of absolute *truth* which then gifts me easy access to peace, power, and freedom.

Knowing this at my core, removes the shackles around a life sentence of paralysis and gives me the hope and incentive to practice clean living on all levels.

A Thought to Ponder at Dawn

Integrity is an awakened state where synchronicity exists between words and deeds.

My full commitment to living in integrity opens my eyes to see where my integrity is still lacking.

This is a golden opportunity for me to choose to put a correction in place and restore integrity once again.

When I see my life as a game, where I'm the main character, taking 100% responsibility for how life will turn out, I am more mindful of choosing which perspective works best.

A Thought to Ponder at Dusk

Feeling alone is an illusion of separation which can produce more fear and instability.

This unbalanced state often throws the identity into survival mode.

The resulting behavior and action are often credible and validated by past interpretations.

Loving thoughts, however, will summon kindness and compassion, thereby diminishing or neutralizing fear, and giving rise to a peaceful calm after the storm.

A Thought to Ponder at Dawn

Suffering occurs when I feel powerless from being at the effect of my perception.

Being accountable for my self-manufactured views makes it more appealing to create new thoughts which nourish me.

There is nothing to fix or do about it except to watch things transform on their own.

A Thought to Ponder at Dusk

Any sign of being upset about anything, whether large or small, is proof that hidden *truth* is lurking somewhere inside of my mind which has yet to be spotlighted.

Although my mind will want to quickly try to fix it, there's nothing to do except allow and accept it until it goes away on its own.

A Thought to Ponder at Dawn

I have the potential to be the transformation that I care to see in my world.

Although I understand that other views exist, I can no longer hold other people responsible for my health and well-being because I'm not a victim of circumstance.

I take ownership of my life and hold no one to no circumstance accountable.

I am the creator of my reality, I am the source of my joy and pain, and I will be mindful of this every day of my life.

A Thought to Ponder at Dusk

My mind is the creator of all illusions.

When I slip focus, I am then at the effect of my environment and have surrendered my center of power to someone or something other than me. Recognizing this dynamic as a first step is not enough to embody self-love and sustainably return to peace.

I, therefore, promise to take whatever action is needed to reclaim my power center. I will practice being mindful of this until it is second nature.

A Thought to Ponder at Dawn

I set my intentions each morning to create a day of my own design.

I allow myself to be inspired by my thoughts and at times, by the thoughts of others.

Although all thoughts are an illusion, I enjoy creating powerful ones which suit me well.

When a thought is not empowering, I can create another from the sea of infinite reality.

A Thought to Ponder at Dusk

Brilliant minds have created the diagnosis, the meanings and commentary, and the prescribed treatments for all documented dis-eases.

A mind also creates meaningful thoughts of joy, sorrow, or any reality it chooses, when it's aware of who the creator is.

My mind is the official home of my identity and *I*, on the other hand, am not my mind.

I am a *spirit* who lives temporarily inside of my mind and body. Has my mind served *me* today or have *I* been bound by its current reality?

A Thought to Ponder at Dawn

Masterminding is an artistic practice that illustrates an ability to create and manifest things that otherwise wouldn't have been possible. It draws from a place of inspiration and infinite possibility where my *illumination* helps it to see more clearly.

A mastermind takes charge from a place of respecting where inspiration comes from, even when it doesn't fully comprehend. The mastering mind has a strong sense of self and corroborates its thought processing with me — the *spirit* within. Wisdom comes to a mastermind when it knows who *I am*.

A Thought to Ponder at Dusk

Without a whole bunch of networked, collective agreements, including my own, my identity would have little or no significance or meaning.

I feel vulnerable to think that I'm not in control of who and what others think of me and yet realize that it's literally none of my business what lurks inside of their minds.

Although I have no say over someone's opinion of me, I do have a full say about mine.

Many of my views still come from my past, some of which are obsolete, and yet, I remain committed to recreating a beautiful reflection of the person I want to be right now.

A Thought to Ponder at Dawn

I can't fix my reality, but I can enlighten it.

I promise to take every opportunity to be objective and honor my subjective point of view as well.

I embrace who and what I am with dignity and grace while allowing myself to evolve and grow, knowing that there are endless possibilities of realities from which to choose.

I do this with integrity because the quality of my life depends upon it.

A Thought to Ponder at Dusk

There is something rarer than unrealized talent, it's the ability to recognize unrealized talent.

All I must do is keep my eyes and heart open to people, places and things.

I am also able to draw on my gut senses when I seek greater insight.

Day 43

A Thought to Ponder at Dawn

Humans are part of the earth's animal kingdom and yet we think differently by thinking that homo sapiens are part of a different animal kingdom classification.

During times of global stress when our humanity for each other seemed to disappear, a National Geographic photo went global illustrating an Orangutan extending his hand to help a human being out of a swamp.

It's nice to see small acts of kindness extended across specie lines, bridging the illusion of a gap that's always there.

"What can I do every day which illustrates my intention of kindness and humanity?"

A Thought to Ponder at Dusk

A tree, a toad, and a hawk are clueless about who they are, yet the tree knows to stand tall and spread its branches, the hawk knows to nest in its branches, and the toad knows to burrow under the fallen leaves.

Innate and instinctual behavior such as this mirrors inner wisdom which surpasses intellect.

We have given up much of our natural instincts to live in society. It is always time to go fishing, camping, or just for a walk in the woods to reset my mind.

A Thought to Ponder at Dawn

Sometimes an expression of loving someone is to offer them a new perspective before they default to the exact behavior which sourced their challenge in the first place.

Seeing the possibility of choices oftentimes makes all the difference and is a priceless gift to give when presented with loving intention.

I remain mindful of this so that I may assist when the opportunity presents itself.

A Thought to Ponder at Dusk

Noticing that when I listen to someone, it's usually to respond first with good intention and also with something of value, but not just to listen and learn.

Being aware of being kinder and more effective, I can choose to listen with only the intention of understanding and not respond at all.

Sometimes people just want to be heard and understood and have that be their contribution. So to be sure of what kind of listening is wanted, I can begin by listening to understand, and then wait to see if there's a question that comes afterward.

It works every time!

A Thought to Ponder at Dawn

I experience countless things and only live inside of my singular interpretation of them.

I realize that each experience is pure, in and of itself, and I'm the one who chooses to either like it, not like it, or take a neutral position towards it.

I am empowered to be fully responsible for *everything* in my life.

A Thought to Ponder at Dusk

The moments that I behave in ways that are loving, kind, compassionate, and playful, I am filled with all of those intentions.

When the light bulb goes on and stays on, I am unstoppable in creating some great beliefs and views about everyone and everything in my life.

I allow this awareness to live inside every cell of being.

A Thought to Ponder at Dawn

Language both coins and limits my reality, but it's all I've got … or is it?

Some ways to communicate which extend beyond language and bridge the great divide are through music, art, and meditation or prayer.

Exploring various styles of music, looking at different expressions of art, and deepening my meditation practice or daily prayers, broadens my perspective on how I communicate.

I can play with language and see how well I do at trying to generate something new. Instead of saying, 'good morning', perhaps I might say something like, 'Make today a day of your own design," or "May your day be everything that you intend it to be."

A Thought to Ponder at Dusk

Collective agreements are real, valid, meaningful, and significant, yet still never true.

Realizing the world of agreement in which I live, helps me to create my expression from what is possible. My freedom to express myself is almost limitless because realities are infinite.

However, when I'm in sync with others, things tend to flow more smoothly.

A Thought to Ponder at Dawn

All that is real to me occurs when my mind perceives it, understands it, and interprets it.

After I gather information and knowledge, I do my best to assimilate it into my life.

I am the only one responsible and accountable for creating my reality because I'm the last one I say good night to and the first I say good morning to.

A Thought to Ponder at Dusk

Self-realization helps position an enlightened soul on a final frontier to no longer needing a human experience.

Whether we believe or don't believe in reincarnation, both vantage points exist and are real and valid.

For believers, when expanded consciousness in a human form is sustainable, the spirit vibrates formlessly throughout eternity. No one knows this for sure and is therefore something to entertain the mind best.

Paying attention to the life that I'm now creating is my primary focus.

A Thought to Ponder at Dawn

The practice of enlightening the mind encourages peace in allowing and accepting people and things as they are, as well as realizing that everything is always, just as it is and does require fixing.

Don't be fooled, however, because the illusory need to fix things is very strong, quite powerful and plants many seeds for dis-eases of the mind. When I can see and better understand these dynamics, I will never again choose to buy into the madness of the multi-billion-dollar world of self-help programs that attempt to fix us from our view of not being good enough.

Imagine a transformed world where financial prosperity is built on authentic growth and development instead of repairing.

A Thought to Ponder at Dusk

Although said with good intention, consider that wishing someone 'good luck', undermines them by failing to acknowledge their ability, as the actual reason for their success. (reread slowly until this sinks in)

On the other hand, wishing someone 'good intentions', helps to summon their awareness and capability, reinforcing their capacity and good intention.

A Thought to Ponder at Dawn

When my mind sees and knows that *I am* a *spirit*, it can allow and accept *me* as the priceless contribution that *I am*.

I'm not the one with a role to play, a purpose to create, a path to walk, or a job to do.

I am consciousness, a *light*, and a beautiful *being*, that when seen by *my* mind, alters its reality on a physiological level.

A Thought to Ponder at Dusk

My mind is the *insistent interpreter* of sensory data, collected by and stored in my brain.

A mind utilizes the brain's limited data, generating a countless array of perspectives.

Underscoring *myself* as the *light* of awareness makes it so much easier for my mind to do its job because it gains greater clarity and efficiency. At best, my mind can only imagine what expansive realities would be created if ever the brain operated at full capacity, instead of only at 10%.

Meditation, clean dieting, listening to Mozart, rest, exercise, deep sleep, and an overall healthier lifestyle, contribute to increasing the brain's functional capacity.

A Thought to Ponder at Dawn

Although I may not realize it at the moment, suffering is completely optional and unnecessary.

Suffering results from unclear, dysfunctional behavior and poor manners when relating. When I forgive myself for thinking that people or things should or shouldn't be a certain way and instead allow and accept what's at hand for being the way that it is, the suffering disappears almost instantaneously.

I privately recall a major life challenge that still causes me to suffer. I now take five minutes, close my eyes and focus on allowing and accepting it to be, just as it is, and expect to watch it quickly vanish.

A Thought to Ponder at Dusk

The potential for sustainable self-realization is available to everyone. The characteristics are simple to understand although not easy to acquire or everyone would be walking around enlightened and there would finally be peace on earth.

When my mind stops resisting or fighting with the natural order of things, it will realize that it was never given the power or ability to control life's powerful energetic flow. Like everything and everyone, I too am made up of stardust. I allow myself to fully embrace this knowledge and allow the seriousness and significance of my beliefs to de-energize and take their proper places.

A Thought to Ponder at Dawn

One of the greatest challenges in life *is* dealing with the persistent masquerade of *truth*, a word that has drastically altered the course of our history.

Without the distinction called 'truth', there may have been much more play, fun, and freedom of expression with little judgment. This is a strong contributor to why sustainable transformation is difficult.

It's an *ultimate* failure to think that any part of my life is absolutely *true* and letting it go, gives me access to all that is possible and enables me to create a life of my own intentions.

A Thought to Ponder at Dusk

History is defined as the period between the beginning of time and up to just a moment ago.

The instant a thought becomes conscious, it's in the past and seated somewhere in history.

One of the greatest ironies in life is to realize that although I exist in the present moment, and dream and plan for the future, my thoughts are generated from my past interpretations. I am in the moment when I am in stillness, quietness, and mindlessness.

A Thought to Ponder at Dawn

The average recognition time for when a thought occurs is just after it has already been created and formed.

When a thought is being created, however, it is developed in the now moment. Thought energy exists before a thought is generated and the mind becomes aware.

With practice, the awareness of *thought energy* is recognizable before a thought is formed and I have the final say on whether to allow it into consciousness or put it into words. When is the last time I witnessed the creation of my thought process?

A Thought to Ponder at Dusk

The more I search, the more I realize that I don't know because whatever I discover pales in comparison to the vastness of infinite intelligence.

Discoveries pull my focus and attention away from the process of inquiry. Inquisition itself is a master key for continuous expansion.

Scientists who are authentically devoted to their scientific area of study, place more focus on the study and not on what is interpreted or documented. The countless changes and upgrades made to historical scientific data insinuate the high probability of either inaccurate assessments or the inability to completely explore the full scope of the research. I can apply the process of discovery as I enter my dream state.

A Thought to Ponder at Dawn

I will not allow the stories from yesterday's news to infiltrate my mind-space of today's current events.

Although this refocus is easier said than done, it opens the space for new possibilities.

I will look to create my day today and be mindful not to pull from yesterday's drama.

A Thought to Ponder at Dusk

A *breakthrough* is a term that defines the moment of an immediate shift in awareness. Thoughts and feelings are instantly redirected from one reality to another and are usually accompanied by an epiphany and/or a noteworthy sense of gratitude. A new view allows for new behavior and action to be taken that would otherwise not have been possible.

Question: When was the last time I had a breakthrough, and can I recall how my entire mind and body felt during that day?

I remember that a breakthrough follows a breakdown and will do my best to not resist being uncomfortable because it doesn't last long before a breakthrough appears. It might just be time to create the space for a breakthrough today!

A Thought to Ponder at Dawn

Reality is a life-long illusion, often grossly mistaken for *truth*.

Productive navigation through my life is to see my illusions as just that… illusions. Achieving thoughtlessness through meditation, however, helps to create a temporary absence of reality if and when a break is needed.

Thoughtlessness brings awareness to the *is-ness* and vibration of *all that is* and is authentically representational of what we'd call the *truth* while in a human experience. Without thought, that which is, *is* the experience itself (*experience* is a synonym for *is-ness* and *truth*), while with thought, there is only our interpretation of the experience and hence, our reality of it.

A Thought to Ponder at Dusk

Knowledge is interpreted information that is collectively agreed upon. It is a collective perspective, that is bestowed with credibility and integrity until something new comes along to either expand upon it or replace it altogether.

With limited resources available, I do my best in every given moment. This gifts me solace from the universal opinion that people are either broken or not good enough, when in fact just like everyone, I always give my best effort in any given moment.

A Thought to Ponder at Dawn

Ironically, communication is a mind's masterful way for me to understand, interpret and seek agreement, inside of an internal illusory world that I mistakenly believe exists outside of my mind.

Although it seems quite convincing, and people would swear by it that there is an *out there*; the *out there* is all made up in my head.

Taking this perspective throughout the day, every day increases my odds for new and expansive mindsets to appear.

A Thought to Ponder at Dusk

Whether it's about how to make a delicious spaghetti sauce or understanding the creation of a brand-new solar system in the cosmos, whether or not I contribute to it or adopt it, every single interpretation and speck of reality is created masterfully inside of my mind.

No doubt there is an outside stimulus and what is made up about it begins in our mind.

The irony is that while a three-foot stick is a measuring stick to me and a play toy to a large dog, the stick hasn't a clue that it's a stick!

The only reason that it's a stick is that I've agreed with a collective agreement.

A Thought to Ponder at Dawn

Mindful living is knowing that I am always exactly where *I am to be* in every moment.

If that were not the case, I'd be somewhere else and probably thinking the same thing.

I place this on a shelf in my mind for easy access every time I feel something should be different from the way it is.

I will move forward today to remain awake to that wisdom.

A Thought to Ponder at Dusk

In the depth of the stillness and silence of *being one with* the continual stream of *now* moments during my meditation, I come to know eternity.

Eternity doesn't only occur after I leave my body, eternity has been going on for quite some time now… an eternity to be exact.

I can say that I'm living inside of eternity now.

Therefore, on a cellular level, *I am* eternity when I'm laser focused on my life force - my breath.

A Thought to Ponder at Dawn

An 'old soul' is the aspect of the mind and body that recognizes that *I am* the *being* who has come to enjoy another *you*-man existence and be in service.

This powerful belief allows me to step into an expanded consciousness as my playground.

A Thought to Ponder at Dusk

Every moment is a new and unchartered experience, despite what my mind thinks.

A bird's flight pattern, even to themselves, is always unique, can never be replicated, and is always occurring in an awakened state of flight.

My walk through life is also unique in every moment and can never be exactly replicated, although my mind seeks to desperately and recklessly reproduce my past.

My mind's resistance to the unknown often stops and sometimes paralyzes me, from being present to the beauty of human exploration. When this fearful behavior ends, the possibility of being fully alive begins.

A Thought to Ponder at Dawn

Until humans arrived on the planet, nothing, including the universe, had any existence. There was no one around to make up the name, *universe,* or associate it with any meaning. Even now, the universe has no idea that it's called a universe, nor has ever existed as such; it simply *is what it is,* whatever that may be. We also created the word, *exist,* giving meaning and validation to it, so that all things that we perceive can then be validated.

Mankind is therefore solely responsible for interpreting the existence of the entire cosmos and everything in it for that matter. It is all quite real, very significant, and holds millennia of documented meaning. The cosmos and all told, exists only inside of my mind.

A Thought to Ponder at Dusk

Time and space are illusions that often go unnoticed as such, allowing our focus to usually be placed on the end game or a place to get to, instead of being present in each moment.

Without the concept of time or space, life on earth would be unrecognizable. Noting that all migrating animals in the wild know when it's appropriate to do so - not one species looks at a clock, knows what day it is, or even worries about how old it is. Believing that we live in the *real* world, animals live in a completely different world that is real and works more efficiently. Devoted meditation allows for *time or space* to dissolve and for only a short time in my life, it allows me to be much more flexible with the reality that I choose to make up.

A Thought to Ponder at Dawn

With integrity, nothing really matters. Without integrity, nothing really matters.

When I'm aware, awake, and have a good handle on my center of power, it doesn't matter to me what is happening in areas in which I have little or no influence. On the other hand, when I'm out of integrity, it's virtually impossible to have things materialize in a way that serves me or others.

Integrity is in place when my awareness of who *I am* is strong, whole, and indivisible. Respecting and honoring my thoughts and spoken words as a mirrored reflection of who I am and what I stand for, lets me know that I am awake. No one needs to second-guess me or anyone who has integrity.

A Thought to Ponder at Dusk

People in need of healing who don't yet realize it, often find other people and circumstances offensive, and chances are, they've lost their center of power and fallen victim to their perceptions.

I choose compassion and kindness because their circumstances unknowingly have a strong hold on their power center.

They may not be open to any outside advisement that would otherwise help; therefore my approach is to be kind, listen to understand, and allow them to shift when they are ready.

A Thought to Ponder at Dawn

A powerful mind is fully responsible and accountable for *everything* that it thinks and believes because it knows that it is responsible for having created it.

It's always a good time to look at the thoughts and beliefs which have caused dis-ease and then recreate them with something that will generate a greater sense of self and allow gratitude to be present for all of the gifts which life has already provided.

A Thought to Ponder at Dusk

I realize that exploration and discovery are not part of my routine. However, expanding my mind and being open to discovery, allows me to practice living inside of inquisition and wonder, rather than any perceived solid results.

Self-reflection on my mind's level of flexibility allows me to sleep easier at night.

Day 61

A Thought to Ponder at Dawn

When the illusion of hidden *truths* is uncovered and recognized, truth vanishes, and reality takes its proper place.

I always have the opportunity to recreate a new reality when the powerless confines of any perceived *truth* are gone.

Knowing that *realities* are limitless, I can choose one that works for me and bid farewell to those that do not serve my highest and greatest good.

A Thought to Ponder at Dusk

A normal mind says: 'When everything is well, I will be happy.'

An enlightened mind says: 'I choose to be happy now and all is well, always'.

I'm aware that external situations and money can surely make life easier and more fun. However, choosing happiness is an internal matter and a powerful state of mind in which no one other than me has the final say.

A Thought to Ponder at Dawn

Mindfulness is a way of being, making things simple to better understand, yet challenging to achieve.

Observing life with indifference, for instance, allows an awakened mind to be fully present and engaged, yet remain neutral in its mindset.

This is one of our greatest challenges and our greatest achievements.

If this were easy to accomplish, we all would have done so, and our world would be unrecognizable in a most amazing way.

Mindfulness is my lifestyle practice and something I encourage in others.

A Thought to Ponder at Dusk

When my mind awakens, it recognizes the impact of the body's impermanence and realizes all its made-up judgments and evaluations.

My mind can then come to grips with understanding reality as the illusion it is and bow in humble service to *me - the spirit, the light, and the observer*, on the path to enlightenment.

A Thought to Ponder at Dawn

Transforming moments occur in the *now*.

They are a result of having a clearer understanding of things that were once thought to be *true*, and a willingness to allow choosing a new reality to take hold.

A Thought to Ponder at Dusk

Authentic self-love is a practice, a way of life, and the only good choice for being available to express unconditional love to anyone around me.

My commitment to authentic love can only stand the test of time when those who have been unkind to me are loved by me, just the same.

If I can count these folks on my two hands, there's no need to write them down, otherwise, it's time for me to grab a pen and paper.

Note: Authentic Love has nothing to do with liking someone, nor does it mean that any interaction with them is necessary.

A Thought to Ponder at Dawn

When my mind is awake, it is often quiet and ready to be in the flow of giving and receiving.

When my mind is thinking, it is often filled with thoughts that may hinder the flow, and so I need to be more mindful.

When I am in a state of mindlessness, there is bliss.

A Thought to Ponder at Dusk

Thinking from a completely new perspective requires persistence and repetition because the challenge to sustain thoughts is new, unfamiliar, and not yet habitual.

One great advantage is that a new vantage point often inspires the generation of new realities that otherwise would have never been made possible.

Day 65

A Thought to Ponder at Dawn

It is wise to understand that not everything I currently think is the reality to choose as my own, especially when I can select from an infinite sea of thought.

By holding myself to account for having chosen my reality, I can change my mind at any time to allow a richer flow and quality of life to continue.

A Thought to Ponder at Dusk

Before anything or anyone is assigned a word and an associated meaning, there is little, if any, value or significance to that particular thing.

Thinking about who I was the moment *before* I was given a family name along with inherited beliefs, makes me wonder what life would be like for me or anyone if, from birth, we were allowed to be our own expression of spirit until we created our own reality.

To date, no one has ever had that opportunity. As I close my eyes for sleep, I will challenge myself to be a newborn infant who is an unencumbered self-loving spirit of God and the Universe and see where that takes me.

A Thought to Ponder at Dawn

There is no way to know how to relate to anything until someone first makes it up by giving it a word, a meaning, and then seeking collective agreement.

Knowing that everything is temporary, I have the power to choose and create an extraordinary life, every moment of every day, and welcome in the great unknown.

By remaining conscious of this, I continue on the road to mastering my center of power.

A Thought to Ponder at Dusk

Allowing myself to fear anything inevitable, like death or growing old, I give it power over me and waste precious time and energy which is non-reimbursable.

Day 67

A Thought to Ponder at Dawn

A breakdown disappears when I surrender whatever *truth* I've been holding onto.

A breakthrough occurs when I reclaim my power to create a new perspective and belief.

I look forward to allowing my *truths* to melt away into reality.

A Thought to Ponder at Dusk

Without any language or associated meanings for people, places, or things, they may still exist, but there's no way for me to relate to any of them.

Language and collective agreements make it possible to express myself and to thrive inside of my own reality and oftentimes the collective reality to which I've agreed.

A Thought to Ponder at Dawn

Words and meanings help give voice to my reality, so choosing them wisely is important. Before learning to speak and communicate, ignorance blanketed my inability to relate.

In human reality, I seek to belong to a community, make a difference, and be validated. Music and melody without words are universal ways to communicate without language.

Breakdowns from limited language and poor communication cause more upset than good and our lack of mastery of these methods, begs us to lead with kindness and compassion.

A Thought to Ponder at Dusk

Instead of going out to look for love, I can also consider examining the internal blockages that are holding me back from just being the love that I'm in search of.

This requires me to have intense focus and attention, as well as mindfulness of the boomerang effect, once I've allowed myself to be the beacon of light that attracts the love that I am.

A Thought to Ponder at Dawn

Initially, my identity will quietly judge people, places, and things, and believe that my assessment is *truly* the way it is. This is how all minds work and is honestly not for me to take personally, even though I may at times.

Fabricating judgments and opinions are simply what my mind does to gain greater understanding; any assessment mistaken as *truth* is a major faux pas.

Recognizing this dynamic allows me the wiggle room needed to play with everything that I make up about anyone or anything.

A Thought to Ponder at Dusk

My identity, along with a major part of my Belief System, was waiting for me long before I was born.

Every newborn's identity is a customized build-out of familial beliefs and traditions which are bestowed upon us without our awareness or consent, and we grow up thinking that it's just the way that it is.

Many people often spend the rest of their lives either living happily inside of these beliefs or doing their best to find a way to free themselves from those beliefs which bind them. There is never a need to dissolve the stronghold on beliefs that are good and serve us, but we surely can seek to alter the ones that don't

A Thought to Ponder at Dawn

Whenever my interpretation of an experience becomes the way that it is, there is an embedded *truth* living somewhere inside of my subconscious that has taken away my power and freedom to choose a new perspective.

This is often the case when I find myself upset, no matter how big or small the upset might be.

Wisdom is knowing that I always have the option to alter my reality by choosing another one that has a higher vibration and will better serve me.

A Thought to Ponder at Dusk

My reality is right, valid, meaningful, real, significant, and provides me with the quality of my life.

I'm forever thankful that nothing, in reality, is *true* or I'd never be able to make the slightest bit of adjustment when there's obsolescence or a time for something new.

True implies that it can never be any other way, or it was never *true*, to begin with.

A Thought to Ponder at Dawn

A child's mind is automatically wired for wonder, exploration, discovery, and knowledge. Although wisdom is said to accompany age, the sense of newness and exploration is often substituted by factual and seemingly concrete beliefs which divert the course for wisdom.

Wisdom recognizes that there is newness and wonder in every second of every day. One of the greatest, yet avoidable pitfalls in the aging process is to think that we *know* or have *mastered* something because that would be more in line with intellectual arrogance.

Wisdom realizes that life is in a flow of continuous streaming of new moments. Choosing to have a Zen Mind, Beginner's Mind allows wonder, newness, and imagination to blanket and inspires us at any age.

A Thought to Ponder at Dusk

No matter how hard I try, although I can't change the people around me, I can change the people around me quite easily instead.

It's always important for me to be responsible for the environment that I choose to live in.

A Thought to Ponder at Dawn

One unique facet of being awake is that my mind has the opportunity to see itself think.

This is a great advantage because not only does it allow me to be introspective about my interpretations of past experiences, but it also allows me to see firsthand the dynamics at play while my mind processes the experience itself.

My mind sees things much more clearly when it knows that *I am* the *light*.

A Thought to Ponder at Dusk

To recognize, acknowledge, and embrace me as the *spirit/light* which lives inside of my physical body, is to know the loving *spirit* that resides inside of every living being.

A Thought to Ponder at Dawn

The practice of authentic self-love includes accepting and allowing my life, my reality, and my thoughts, to be exactly where they are and not making them wrong in any given space and time.

Going with the flow of life allows me to refocus my mind on being awake instead of being concerned with the pace and stream of life itself. I choose to have fun allowing myself to flow with life's stream whether it's smooth and calm or if it's like rafting the roaring rapids — it's all good.

A Thought to Ponder at Dusk

For every cause, there is an effect, and for every action, a reaction.

Causes and actions are constituents of creation itself, both of which have no claim or interest in any of the outcomes.

Action taken to create a specific effect or desired reaction requires premeditation and sometimes focused intention and is only created by living beings, oftentimes for survival.

The cosmos, on the other hand, holds no calculations, allowing nature to find its way.

A Thought to Ponder at Dawn

God is considered to be the Creator and Manifestor of all that is *un-manifest*.

Anything which has manifested is therefore a creation *of* God and is *not* God itself. Spending too much time on the incomprehensible is silly when there is so much of human life to create.

Whether or not I find out after I leave my body is irrelevant in the scheme of things when I can *carpe diem* - seize the day - every day. I create an incredible day for myself and realize that although I didn't initially create my identity, I can create whatever I choose as I govern my life.

A Thought to Ponder at Dusk

The magnitude and intensity of any upset resulting from failed expectations are directly proportional to the energetic investment that I've made.

The magnitude and intensity of all joys stemming from exceeding my expectations are directly proportional to the energetic investment I've put into it.

Bottom line? I promise myself to invest in each day wisely.

A Thought to Ponder at Dawn

At birth, in all of its wonder, my young and inquisitive mind soaked in as much information as possible and found ways in which to relate to people, places, and things.

My older mind is fuller, often seeking to clear out the clutter of accumulated, antiquated information, to live more simply and peacefully.

Meditation gives me needed mind space from years of stimulus overload and helps me to return to the innocence of a Zen Mind and enjoy each moment as new again.

My devoted meditation helps me to clear out the clutter.

A Thought to Ponder at Dusk

Although it is perfectly OK to *not* be OK when things are *not* OK, one of the greatest gifts is when I find myself completely and authentically OK when things are *not* OK.

If this was an easy dynamic to achieve, everyone would be authentically OK, regardless.

My commitment to remaining awake allows this to be possible.

A Thought to Ponder at Dawn

There are many ways to view my world, and choosing negative perspectives doesn't make things any more *truth-full* that choosing to harbor positive thoughts, not when I can passionately create my world as I desire.

Once I realize that I'm the one making up everything, I can instantly choose to embrace another reality.

In the world of imagination inside of my mind, who else but I am responsible? (that's really not a question and Walt Disney was a perfect example of this)

A Thought to Ponder at Dusk

An over-crowded mind can short-circuit itself as a result of overwhelming.

A busy mind is filled with valid interpretations, yet a portion still has unnecessary clutter.

A quiet mind is a calm and peaceful space where thoughts can flow smoothly.

An empty mind is a thoughtless mind and a doorway to blissful heaven on earth reality.

Day 77

A Thought to Ponder at Dawn

My awareness of the *'isness'* of anything being just *as it is - the experience itself* - and knowing that all meanings of things are fictitious, allows me to understand the pure existence of an experience itself, finally realizing the improbability of relating to anything without it having been assigned a meaning. (reread until fully understood)

My interpretation of an experience holds the associated power from the meaning that it was given and is a wake-up call for me to bear the responsibility for any disempowering interpretation I've created.

My daily challenge is to see where I feel disempowered and what interpretation I placed upon that particular experience.

A Thought to Ponder at Dusk

I turn my wrist inward and point my finger at the person responsible for creating the only world I've ever known; the world in which I live exists only inside of my mind.

Gaining collective agreement of my perceived outside world will not take ownership or blame away from me for having created my vantage point.

A Thought to Ponder at Dawn

A Very Short Timeline: First I am born, then hopefully I live a healthy and qualitative life, followed by me leaving my body in worse shape than I had found it.

I spend countless days of my life painting my perspectives on life's empty canvas and holding significant meanings, which I oftentimes forget, holds no *truth*.

Although everything is an illusion, I can still make sure to have great integrity in my life.

A Thought to Ponder at Dusk

Having a tight hold on my interpretations, which produces every bit of my reality, paralyzes any chances of creating a new perspective and seals off access to freedom and happiness; maintaining a white-knuckled grip is not on an 'A' list of best practices.

A Thought to Ponder at Dawn

An experience is a pure energetic occurrence. The mind then instantly interprets that energy vibration into *thought energy*, and then goes on to create a *real thought*, about it, aka. *reality*.

With devoted practice, I can gain an appropriate level of sensitivity necessary to recognize and determine whether or not a particular thought energy is worth holding onto or if discarding it is a healthier option before my mind turns it into a real thought.

A Thought to Ponder at Dusk

Although an experience can never be changed or altered, my perspective and interpretation of the experience certainly can.

Considering each year of my life to be a chapter in my autobiography, I'd destroy the book if I ripped out any of the pages from earlier chapters.

Therefore, I will begin writing and living from a place of possibility and new perspectives. Allowing and accepting things to be as they are, offers a smooth transition into my next chapter bearing little resemblance to prior chapters.

A Thought to Ponder at Dawn

Wisdom is realizing that I'm always connected to *all that is*, was, and ever will be, especially when my mind thinks otherwise.

Holding the space that I am *spirit, soul, individual consciousness*, or whatever there is to call *me*, my mind uses my light to become more en-'light'ened and awakened.

A Thought to Ponder at Dusk

When mindfulness is present, being part of a community is generated from selflessness.

Surrounding myself with like-minded energetic individuals is one of those blissful realities which I feel on occasion.

Belonging to communities that support my passions allows my life to thrive.

Day 81

A Thought to Ponder at Dawn

As the *translator* of data and images that are collected by my brain, my mind's built-in programming retrieves, assimilates, and shares stored realities via standard methods of communication.

Filled with information that is mostly antiquated and yet useful, my mind uses its resources to navigate and connect with others.

Note: there's nothing wrong with antiquated stories, quite the contrary - history majors would agree.

A Thought to Ponder at Dusk

My brain is like a computer hard drive and my mind is the program itself which requires periodic updating.

Intrinsic in all technology, the mind included, there appears to be built-in obsolescence unless, of course, it continually upgrades itself with new and improved data.

This is why adults who continue learning, experimenting, creating, and remaining active, are healthier and live longer happier lives.

Tangential note - Oftentimes while filling out forms and such, who'd have ever thought a computer would check to see if you were human?

A Thought to Ponder at Dawn

My mind has created an identity that continuously argues for a position to understand, evaluate, fix, improve, and control things in its environment.

My mind takes its job seriously and is oftentimes stubborn and bel-belligerent about holding onto its vantage point. Expanding my mental awareness, however, helps to neutralize subconscious thoughts of obligation and burden allowing a sense of greater ease and inner peace to be possible. My mind is like no other and functions optimally with self-loving thoughts.

A Thought to Ponder at Dusk

Although infinite intelligence makes everything possible, my mind's perceptions place unintentional, sometimes unkind, limitations and boundaries on what's possible.

It often takes a serious life challenge or a devoted practice of mindless meditation to see the actual *possibility* of possibility itself, otherwise, we remain blind. Being attached or reactive to people, situations, or things is unnecessary because I always have free will to choose a new perspective, because it's totally up to me.

There is great freedom knowing that while I am temporarily here in a human earth suit, I'm able to create realities that produce the best of times while I'm here! I now create new stuff daily and send my past dysfunctional interpretations to the garbage heap.

A Thought to Ponder at Dawn

Babies and young children are the embodiment of beautiful, free, and unencumbered spirit energy — this is one reason why their physical scent is so appealing and why they're so adorable to be around, not to mention the beauty of their innocence and vulnerability.

Until passed beliefs are fused into them, a child's mind remains untouched and pure. Adults with all good intentions will impart inherited and historical information into their minds.

This passed-down information will be both wonderful and toxic, altering their innocence. All initial information, positive or negative, greatly impacts a young mind's yearning to connect and relate.

A Thought to Ponder at Dusk

An enlightened mind embodies love, compassionate understanding, and equanimity.

An enlightened mind no longer *has* to do anything and yet, will do just about anything in the name of love and kindness.

What thoughts before slumber will better welcome both self-love and kindness?

A Thought to Ponder at Dawn

Things often happen by chance, yet the reasons produced as explanations are literally and instantly conjured up during the hindsight of what just happened.

A powerful awakening moment occurs when my mind realizes that it creates and accepts all its reasons as *true* when they never are.

Facing the fear that my interpretation of things isn't true requires courage.

Whether or not my reality is correct is less important than my mind being flexible, lucid, and open.

A Thought to Ponder at Dusk

Before we came into existence and immediately after our extinction, the universe will no longer have any meaning or significance to itself or relate to anyone or anything.

The universe is neither empty nor void because those words are also made-up concepts. A more accurate attempt at a description of what happens is to say that I come from and return to the formless *is-ness* that *I am* because I am neither my mind nor my body.

Assimilating this into consciousness is a big deal and has great implications.

A Thought to Ponder at Dawn

From birth, my mind came with the capacity potential to collect and store beliefs and stories which were assumed to be helpful to navigate me throughout life.

I'm in awe when I look at how my brain and mind are designed and relate to each other, they are unique for sure.

Ironically enough, however, the vast assortment of life's creations is a result of evolutionary advancement that is designed without any motivating beliefs or reasons. Throughout space and time whenever possible life itself finds a way to create itself, adapt to survive, and thrive and flourish.

What will I create today for myself and generate out from nowhere?

A Thought to Ponder at Dusk

Being mindful that I am the cause of my reality deepens my sense of self-realization.

Full realization may take a lifetime(s) to achieve and will occur in that moment's time.

The key to sustainable enlightenment is when a mind's relationship to all that is real, remains neutral and nonreactive.

A Thought to Ponder at Dawn

Serendipity arrives when my awareness expands and my mind surrenders itself to views of acceptance, allowance, and gratitude.

With free will, focus, and clearer vision, I trust the dynamics in the special network of intellectual consciousness which makes serendipity very real and alive in my daily life.

A Thought to Ponder at Dusk

It's often been said that the best way to learn something is to teach it.

Practicing what I teach allows me to be highly qualified to teach what I practice.

My Daily Mantra:

"The Life that I Lead, is the Lesson I Teach".

Day 87

A Thought to Ponder at Dawn

I have every right to have my own thoughts and not have my thoughts *have* me. My mind adds significant meaning to thoughts because that's just how it's wired.

Looking back, I realize that I've never had an *original* thought before. Most of my thoughts and beliefs are inherited, socially learned, and perpetuated from past thoughts, while perhaps only a handful may have been generated from thoughtlessness.

It's virtually impossible to generate and sustain a brand-new thought while maintaining a healthy mind and functional human reality because my reality is based on history. At best, anything new will continue being generated by the only reality I've ever known.

The essential takeaway here is that I am responsible for it, is all.

A Thought to Ponder at Dusk

Being awake helps to properly nourish and evolve my mind as well as its identity.

As the co-creator of thoughts that form my reality, placing any *truth* into any interpretation is complete silliness at best.

Placing laser focus on my breath welcomes in thoughtlessness and readies my mind for a peaceful and beautiful reset.

A Thought to Ponder at Dawn

An awakened mind recognizes that its wiring is to fix and control its environment and exists inside of a complete illusion that is significantly based on fears of the unknown.

Holding onto this wisdom provides access to the possibility of unbridled freedom. An awakened mind also realizes that although it doesn't have to do anything, there is much that it does end up doing in the name of understanding, contribution, compassion, and love. I will remain as mindful as I can be as I choose to carpe diem.

A Thought to Ponder at Dusk

A greater understanding of how my mind functions provides a general schematic for me to access the infinite awareness of the collective mind as well as greater consciousness.

Although each mind is vastly unique, our human emotions appear to remain universal, the same holds for global collective agreements.

For instance, although it may be called by a different name, sadness, and joy, trees and airplanes, and fish and carnivals, are globally understood because of having the same definition and collective agreement. (Exceptions apply) - the game of 'football' in the US and England are two different things, but we all know that, which is why it works)

Remember: We are All Unique… Just… Like… Everyone… Else.

A Thought to Ponder at Dawn

My brain is a hard-wired organ that seemingly has a limited capacity to collect and store information; for instance, I am unable to hear the high frequencies of sounds that other animals can.

My awakening mind, however, can access infinite intelligence and allow my light — *me* — to help it use the data collected from my brain very differently.

A Thought to Ponder at Dusk

When I stop making things wrong for being the way that they are, my interpretations of people, places, and things are more accurate; gaining this new perspective opens my mind to greater awareness.

I never relate to things the '*way they are*, even when I think I do.

Instead, I see things because of the way that I am, using my wheelhouse of thoughts.

Day 90

A Thought to Ponder at Dawn

Before beginning my day, I will quiet down for two to four minutes so that I may watch the continuous flow of my existing thoughts... just to observe them, nothing more.

Witnessing them brings greater clarity to the streaming of these thoughts. By closing my eyes, I can see that I'm having these thoughts instead of them *having* me.

Said differently, these are not my thoughts but rather the thoughts that are in my head. The greater realization is that I've not been having thoughts, they've been having me.

I realize now that at any time of day, I can recognize thoughts that I don't care for and choose to substitute ones that better suit my growth and development. This priceless shift in perspective allows me to be responsible for my well-being.

A Thought to Ponder at Dusk

Everything is energy which is made up of infinite and highly specialized vibrations. Every thought in my mind, every cell in my body, and every feeling that I have is all energy.

Every choice that I make and action that I take vibrates at a frequency that I can choose to change at any time simply by shifting my focus and the power of my will

A Thought to Ponder at Dawn

My perspective on life significantly alters when I realize that the *outside* world is a result of all interpretations that I hold on to.

Every interpretation that I've ever adopted, created, or currently relate to, has existed inside of my mind without me being responsible for most of it.

Holding myself to account and being aware of what I think and say is a big uphill climb.

I can only imagine the view from the top of that mountain!

A Thought to Ponder at Dusk

The outer world to an extrovert is like being at a drive-in movie where the projected images on the large screen are coming from the projector inside of my mind.

The outer world of an introvert is like being alone in my room watching black and white movies on my cell phone.

This non-genetically, set in stone, perspective gives me the power to choose freely.

A Thought to Ponder at Dawn

My reality is significant at times and often crystal clear to me most of the time. My reality is not always balanced and yet, I do the best I can to find balance. My reality is difficult for others to deal with at times, especially when I'm out of sorts.

My reality is wonderful for people to be around when I am focused and up to good stuff. My reality makes the day fly by so quickly when I'm in service. My reality is always right and yet, never true.

When confronted with being right or being kind, I promise myself to choose kindness.

A Thought to Ponder at Dusk

Holding onto any kind of upset is a function of holding onto my past and keeps me stuck. The degree to which I hold on to upset illustrates the degree of my resistance to growth, and my willingness to allow transformation, and reveals where my commitments are.

Although anxiety is evoked when moving into an uncertain future, holding onto my past quells the expansion of consciousness that I long for. Like the proverbial light that is seen at the end of the dark tunnel when transitioning, freedom, joy, and happiness, are found on the other side of letting go by embracing my fears and pioneering myself into new territory.

A Thought to Ponder at Dawn

I get quiet and still now to enjoy five slow, soft, comfortable breaths before I begin my day.

During each of those breaths, I will set my intentions on calm energy in my inhale.

When finished, I will take five more and breathe in *peace, abundance, inner joy, full contentment,* and *self-love.*

This is morning practice that I choose to take into my day and share with others today.

A Thought to Ponder at Dusk

The absence of *truth* in my life is most rewarding to assimilate because it frees me to upgrade whatever reality I choose, allowing me to watch my consciousness expand.

Taking full responsibility for every chapter in my autobiography, I no longer allow any of the earlier chapters, which were mainly inherited, adopted, and perpetuated by me, to have the charge they once had or any strongly held influence over how my book will end.

A Thought to Ponder at Dawn

When I notice my mind judging others, I'll not look to fix the thoughts but rather embrace them as benign, and avoid myself going down some dramatic, illusory, pathway.

Ultimately, every mind is responsible for the stories they create and share.

Exploring my life challenges and joys allows me to have greater compassion for all minds that create their own illusions.

A Thought to Ponder at Dusk

Our deepest pain is usually the trigger that ignites empowerment and brings a new and more expanded way of thinking into existence.

Since it's not possible to have a breakthrough without having a breakdown, I'm hoping for some shoulder, elbow, and knee pads for my birthday.

A Thought to Ponder at Dawn

There's a huge difference between an experience and my interpretation of that experience.

My new interpretation has nothing to do with any experience and all to do with something I'm relating to from a past perspective.

Although I'll not be able to claim much accountability for what I've done in the past, understanding this more clearly allows me to be fully responsible for creating any future interpretations.

This is a lifestyle that requires keen focus and devotion as part of my practice.

A Thought to Ponder at Dusk

Where will I be in my life and what will I be doing, when I fully assimilate the realization that my identity has been completely inherited, adopted, perpetuated, and all made up?

I'd like to think that I'll be right here and present to a most amazing moment in time as I welcome a new, unreasonable, and unrecognizable, beginning.

A Thought to Ponder at Dawn

I think and pray for people who are not well off and recognize that my life can always be worse than it is.

This allows for a more balanced perspective of reality and deepens my sense of gratitude.

I will now think of three things I'm grateful for and be sure to share that with those I love.

A Thought to Ponder at Dusk

My reality is a byproduct of both collective agreements and my perceptions.

Although reality remains an illusion that bears no truth, it is quite real, meaningful, and oftentimes significant.

Even though my reality will grow and expand, I'll still be left having a reality.

When I take the time to sit back and watch my mind think, I realize that I can actually *have* a reality and not necessarily allow it to *have* me.

A Thought to Ponder at Dawn

When fully realizing that everything has, is, and will always be made up inside of my mind, I have an enormous opportunity of living more freely and powerfully inside of my meaningful illusions authored by me.

I will touch the lives of those I love today by creating something new that I love about them.

A Thought to Ponder at Dusk

I can always tap into happiness when I get still and place my focus on quieting down my mind and body.

Familiarity with inner happiness allows me to create happiness anywhere, at any time.

Happiness is a state of mind, a way of being, and now my default emotion.

I no longer rely on people, places, or things, for my happiness.

A Thought to Ponder at Dawn

When sadness or any kind of discontent comes to mind, I will ask myself, "Why have I chosen to give my power away and blame my upset on something or someone especially since I've created that lame-duck interpretation in the first place?

All discontentment is a result of a failed expectation that my mind has created.

By reconfiguring my expectations, I can alter my reality.

A Thought to Ponder at Dusk

Whenever life becomes chaotic and appears to be crumbling all around me, I will remind myself that things are actually shifting and falling into place instead and that all is well.

A Thought to Ponder at Dawn

When I choose to no longer take part in the kind of *freedom of speech* that is hurtful, vengeful, cruel, nasty, or mean to others, I'm able to set a new precedent from which to approach others without exception.

This is the doorway to realizing unconditional love.

A Thought to Ponder at Dusk

When I find myself non-reactive, neutral, and balanced, about something that would have usually ruffled my feathers, I feel a sense of emancipation from being at the effect of that particular circumstance.

With practice, I intend to apply this behavior to every aspect of my life as a new standard.

All major shifts in perspective that I'm able to sustain will impact the quality of my life.

A Thought to Ponder at Dawn

Some people feel the temperature of a raindrop as it touches their skin, while other folks just get wet.

The same rainfall can have different interpretations, the same stimulus, and different responses.

What will it take for me to remain awake to how and what I'm interpreting today as only a function of my mind and not, *the way it is* while doing my best to be non-reactive?

A Thought to Ponder at Dusk

Like it or not, fully understanding that my reality is completely my creation, gives me access to my center of power and my mind's emancipation.

Preventing myself from falling asleep is a great challenge that allows me to gain access to fun and play while enjoying what it feels like to have expanded my consciousness.

These are very sacred moments in time.

A Thought to Ponder at Dawn

The mind not only likes to be right, it likes to let others know that it's right as well.

This is one reason why we sometimes make other people or situations wrong. Somehow the mind is obsessively on a mission and is driven to be the rightest. When mindfulness appears, however, it becomes clear that everyone is in their *right* mind.

Initially deflated by this, a healthy and logical mind has its moment of reconciliation. Being in my right mind doesn't always award me popular consensus because crowd appeal is based on collective agreement whether or not I may disagree, right? ;))

A Thought to Ponder at Dusk

Much like the earth is the planet that we currently call home, the real world is the place that exists inside of my mind.

Without individual minds buying into a collective consensus, holding global agreements about people, places, and things, would not exist as we know them.

A Thought to Ponder at Dawn

Both kindness and gratitude are two of Love's family members, while self-righteousness tends to live a nomadic life.

The instant that I'm aware of myself choosing to be *right* instead of *kind*, I promise myself to clean it up as quickly as possible.

A Thought to Ponder at Dusk

Despite having collective agreements regarding many things because they're essential to relate with others, my point of view is just one of countless vantage points which are in constant flux.

This recognition makes it possible to appreciate everyone else's ever-changing reality as well as my own.

A Thought to Ponder at Dawn

Gaining a new perspective, results from redirecting my mind's awareness onto another thought energy pattern that exists outside of my present and predictable reality.

Shifting a thought is simple to understand and even do, yet it requires intentional focus and repetition for it to become the new default reality; practice, patience, and devotion are essential for me to assimilate and sustain any new vantage point.

A Thought to Ponder at Dusk

I often say that I'm going through something whenever I'm in circumstantial discomfort.

A more authentic view might be for me to realize that I'm *growing* through something instead of going through it.

This is not so much a play on words as it is a refocus of actual intention and integrity.

A Thought to Ponder at Dawn

The mind is driven to understand and relate to whatever it perceives in the outside world.

When I claim full responsibility for my mind, I will sense a power that money cannot buy and recognize that my center of power is always inside of me and will be until I transition.

When I'm unable to feel peace and calm at my core, I will look deeper until I do.

A Thought to Ponder at Dusk

My mind is made up of countless interpretations and agreements.

It perpetuates all learned distinctions like the existence of my body, my soul, and everything I know about life on earth and in the cosmos.

Whenever I make the mistake of thinking there's any *truth* in the collective mind, I'm confined to one vantage point that owns me.

This has been one of humanity's greatest blunders that we still have in common.

A Thought to Ponder at Dawn

While I'm inside my body, my mind will run the Greatest *Reality Show* of a Lifetime.

As an awakened partnership, the trio, aka. my mind, my body, and *Me / spirit*, have a greater chance of having an amazing life filled with gratitude than dealing with all the needless and tiresome drama.

Whenever my mind quiets itself, it knows who *I am*.

A Thought to Ponder at Dusk

When I pay attention, I watch my mind giving meaning and significance to everything; it creates all my joys and sorrows and everything real in my life.

Blessed with the inquisitiveness for exploring the unknown, my courageous and fearful mind will venture to gain an understanding of how and why things are the way they are.

Knowledge allows my mind to have a false sense of control, safety, and comfort at best while also knowing that everything is temporary and in life's constant flow.

A Thought to Ponder at Dawn

My mind is home to my identity which seems solid.

While in deep meditation, I can go out of my mind and gain access to a much greater view of what is possible.

Blessed to know what thoughtlessness is, I have the freedom and resource to recreate a more amazing identity of my own design whenever I so choose.

A Thought to Ponder at Dusk

My mind's current tally of beliefs is the summation of my past interpretations which have helped me to navigate through my life with notable efficiency and ease.

Periodically, I recognize the need for a mental spring cleaning and look to see which old thoughts no longer serve me and need to be filed into the trash bin.

Clearing out the old files and obsolete chatter that no longer serves me, clears the mind of space and makes room for new and more fulfilling thoughts to become real.

A Thought to Ponder at Dawn

Creation is a generative behavior. which comes without any beliefs or reasons and has no history.

Genesis is a God-given attribute because authentic creation comes from nothing.

Although not based on any past circumstances, what I create is oftentimes inspired by past perspectives.

Beginning with an unconventional brain dump into a new bucket list of things I'd love to create, is a good place to begin looking at what passionately excites me.

A Thought to Ponder at Dusk

Being in gratitude is the greatest form of receivership.

Being in service is the greatest form of transmission.

Being mindful allows greater clarity and impact when receiving and transmitting.

Being still and reflective allows me inner peace and joy.

A Thought to Ponder at Dawn

Worrying significantly impacts the body as it destabilizes my power center, wears on my physical strength, and infiltrates my thoughts with stress, upset, and sometimes depression.

Worrying triggers a reactive impulse of withdrawal which often results from some ridiculous or subconscious fear.

While I create my day, I think of a person or situation that I hold worrisome concerns around and recreate new thoughts which will completely alter my day.

A Thought to Ponder at Dusk

A transformational shift from what is possible to what is real requires having a strong focus and intention behind it.

Once this shift occurs, any action following that moment will be reflective of that shift and bear little resemblance to anything that would have occurred otherwise.

A Thought to Ponder at Dawn

When viewed over trillions of years, all of the assumed chaos in the cosmos appears to have an astonishing order unto itself. No matter how awake and intelligent I am, my mind is unable to comprehend the countless number of suns, planets, and universes in space.

To date, it's been proven scientifically that universes are continuously being created and the cosmos is continuously expanding while we focus on our daily life on a little blue dot suspended in space. Having a proper perspective is always a good thing.

A Thought to Ponder at Dusk

Looking at the same peaceful, twinkling, starry sky each night, is a beautiful yet gross illusion.

When I look up into the sky, I'm looking at stars that have long since burned out and are therefore no longer there because it takes many thousands of light years for light to travel through space before it is completely gone.

This explains why newly formed stars and solar systems cannot be seen. This is similar to me looking at my personal history at this very moment. Although my history remains present inside my mind, it's been long gone for some time now, and perhaps it is a good reason for me to allow it to lose its negative charge.

A Thought to Ponder at Dawn

Choosing benevolence over faith would bring divinity to all religions.

A world that is without religion but is filled with loving faith and goodness, would bring unbridled happiness to us all and all the joys of heaven to earth.

A Thought to Ponder at Dusk

There is something rarer than unrealized talent — it is the ability to know unrealized talent when you see it.

Helping others to step into their potentiality is one of the greatest and yet, sometimes thankless gifts that we can give.

When I think of the last time that I helped someone out in a significant manner, it makes me realize how awesome it felt to be me.

A Thought to Ponder at Dawn

There is something rarer than forgiving a wrongdoer — it's the ability to see and embrace the goodness which lies dormant underneath their conflicted set of circumstances.

Those who are unkind or do things that aren't of good intention, are often troubled and usually not open to receiving. Whenever I attempt to assist people in need who are not ready, it's usually not effective.

Allowing them to be right where they are and accepting their set of circumstances at that moment, allows them to feel validated and eventually open to learning something new.

A Thought to Ponder at Dusk

Waiting for things to happen is oftentimes a passive role, or is it?

A cat that waits for a mouse to come out of its hole plays a very active role because they remain in immediate and constant attention.

Unlike how I might wait for things, a cat remains quiet, still, very present, and ready to enjoy its food the moment that lunch arrives.

What would my life look like if I waited with focus, attention, and readiness to act?

A Thought to Ponder at Dawn

The heart is a most precious yet funny-looking organ for what we make it mean. Its purpose is to receive deoxygenated blood on one side and then from the other side, send oxygenated blood throughout the body, bringing it life's energy with each beat.

The mind has created the heart to possess emotions and feelings which reside inside of the mind instead. When we say that the heart either aches or feels deep love, the mind is still a host to those emotions, not the heart.

Although matters of the heart remain inside of the mind, the mind felt it appropriate to give the heart a loving and romantic purpose because of the life force that it provides. This collective belief makes the heart a very real and significant center for emotion.

A Thought to Ponder at Dusk

The *light* which shines in others is who they authentically *are*.

Recollection of this makes it much easier for me to pardon their mind's imperfections and allows me to express my gratitude and compassion towards them.

What people must go on my list for me to apply this awareness?

A Thought to Ponder at Dawn

The ability to continually gain broader perspectives doesn't make me a better person, how I conduct myself does.

What intellectual arrogance, if any, or sense of privilege, might still be lurking inside of my mind, that if I were to give it up completely and for my own good, I'd feel a deepened sense of gratitude and joy?

A Thought to Ponder at Dusk

The moment that ultimate enlightenment arrives, relativity disappears. All of the 4300 (approximate.) earth-based religions that we've created, will continue 'fighting' for their position of credibility and vanish at the doorway to enlightenment on earth or when we leave our bodies.

Although enlightenment waits for everyone on the other side and is better than words can describe or any mind can comprehend, it is available to us all here on earth if we seek it.

A Thought to Ponder at Dawn

The realization of myself being fine and OK, just the way I am in this and every moment, disappears the need to *have to* improve myself.

This allows improvements to organically occur on their own and not because anything that was perceived to be broken needed to be fixed,

A Thought to Ponder at Dusk

Miracles are unknown laws of energy that science has yet to bring understanding too.

Scientific breakthroughs provide explanations that help to remove the associated mysticism from miracles, allowing miracles to transform into known facts.

A Thought to Ponder at Dawn

The only time I will create a new perspective is when I understand that generating a new thought and point of view takes more focused repetition that the original perspective.

I'll guarantee the sustainability of my new reality by promising myself to place integrity in my commitment or until a new and more expansive reality comes along.

A Thought to Ponder at Dusk

When my mind is aware of me being the *spirit* within, it allows my light to shine brightly inside of itself and illuminate dark areas for greater awareness.

A byproduct of mindfulness is having more freedom and joy in my life.

A Thought to Ponder at Dawn

Success is what happens between failed attempts; it's impossible to have success without having failed attempts with which to compare it to.

To be clear, failed attempts are only attempts and do not mean that I am a failure.

In addition, failed attempts are not even closely linked to my sense of self-worth, and to think that way, would be completely incorrect.

Authentic failure does occur, however, whenever I halt all actions towards success it still holds no bearing on any sense of self-worth or image.

A Thought to Ponder at Dusk

I can't fix my blind spots, but I can *enlighten* them.

My mind can create new thoughts when my light brightens the areas of the subconscious, allowing greater space for imagination.

A Thought to Ponder at Dawn

Fearing that which is inevitable, is the silliest of all fears.

Birth, for instance, is an illusory and terminal concept, guaranteeing that no one gets off the planet alive; this is unworthy of any thought time whatsoever.

Whenever I fear living my life full out, I become part of the living dead. Life itself is created by happenstance and any purpose assigned to it is given by me.

Therefore I will take all that is wonderful in my life and embrace it while I give up and pitch all that no longer works for me. Although fear is part of reality, it doesn't have to own me, and therefore promise myself to generate the courage needed to live my life on the edge of my comfort zone.

A Thought to Ponder at Dusk

When my mind steps back and notices itself thinking about whatever it's perceiving, it not only has the chance to see the mechanics of its own thought process, but it can also choose to generate thoughts more wisely.

Choosing nourishing thoughts to think about just before my evening slumber will fuel my mind with thoughts that nourish my mind and body.

A Thought to Ponder at Dawn

Giving up, letting go, and surrendering are three separate things. Giving up requires a sense of resignation and letting go yields away my power.

Surrendering, however, is my mind's way of powerfully choosing to allow a far greater intelligence the permission to take over and lead the way to what's possible, while I remain whole and complete.

I will be mindful to refrain from either giving up or letting go and allow the possibility of surrendering to a far greater intelligence than my own, to lead the way.

A Thought to Ponder at Dusk

A great sense of joy and liberation occurs when *wanting* and *needing* are finally exposed as nothing more than unnecessary, motivating, and compelling illusions, which destabilize me and diminish my power center.

Perhaps the only time they are necessary is when I choose to *want* and *need* for nothing.

A Thought to Ponder at Dawn

Birds are completely unaware that we've turned their wings into a symbol of freedom. Many children often dream of flying with or without having a pair of wings.

Like a bird, I will never have the privilege of knowing the extent to which I have inspired others just by being me. The irony is that whenever I try too hard to inspire others, I often kill off the possibility of inspiring them.

When my focus remains on being passionate about something, others become inspired as they witness something genuine within me which ignites something inside of themselves.

A Thought to Ponder at Dusk

We are all a by-product of our past collective agreements and interpretations. Although quite real and meaningful, the joke is on me to ever believe that the good, the bad, and the insignificant, were ever *true*.

The power of creation and influence which thoughts have underscores being more mindful to maintain my center of power during the creation process. I alone begin and end my day with fabricated thoughts, which I can alter at any time.

A Thought to Ponder at Dawn

Whenever I'm having a rough go of things, it's often because I'm thinking of upsetting, negative, or challenging thoughts. When mindfulness appears, I can immediately stop myself and begin thinking thoughts that empower me.

Since all thoughts are made up anyway, I no longer have to give any credibility to any negative ones which might deplete me in any way.

A Thought to Ponder at Dusk

Today I have done my best to make a difference and contribute to others.

I can rest easy and go to sleep reflecting on my day.

As I go to sleep, I set my intentions to dream of a better tomorrow so that when I awake, I'm prepared to create my day with the appropriate actions needed for that to happen.

Day 121

A Thought to Ponder at Dawn

Before I look forward to great things in my life as possible, I must first realize the bogus untruths about why things weren't possible, to begin with.

Once realized, I will happily wipe the egg off my face for allowing myself to be bamboozled and be able to better understand and take charge of my life more proactively.

I look forward to seeing what running my life, 'my way' looks like.

A Thought to Ponder at Dusk

Although it seems as if there is a road to travel, the *journey* is never about getting to a destination.

I create my path by staying right where I am, inside a raft while enjoying the flow of life's stream and watching things transform before my eyes.

Being more observant helps to bring balance and quality to my life.

A Thought to Ponder at Dawn

There are countless more realities than there are people because realities are infinite.

The path or road which I travel is forged, not followed, and eventually converges with all other roads at the specific endpoint where enlightenment begins.

This is when our temporary time in a human experience is soon over, and we welcome a new existence elsewhere.

A Thought to Ponder at Dusk

The opposite reflection of L-O-V-E is E-V-O-L.

Without darkness, light has no existence.

Generally speaking, without *yin* as the relative opposite, there is no *yang* with which to compare itself to.

A Thought to Ponder at Dawn

What pulls me away from being in a constant state of love, is forgetting who *I am*.

Keeping site of who *I am* is challenged by daily living which pulls my focus and encourages forgetfulness.

When I assimilate into my day-to-day world what it's like to be in a meditative state, I can more easily maintain my power center and know who *I am* at each moment in time.

Sustaining this challenge will be easier by reminding others of their power center. This gives me purpose and satisfaction and helps me to mirror what I teach.

A Thought to Ponder at Dusk

When I am at the *effect* of something, I find myself saying that life is difficult and often plays the role of a victim. When I say that life is awesome, I generate the love that everyone wishes to see in the world.

In addition, Life is Good - Life is Awesome - Life is Worth Living - Life is Worth My Time... even when I don't think or feel that way... it's that simple!

A Thought to Ponder at Dawn

As an infant, I was happy when I was happy and sad when I was sad. I was simply living in the moment.

As an adult, whenever I struggle to accept and allow sadness to be as it is, I do my best to fix the discomfort as quickly as possible. At some point, I forget that all relative opposites are an intrinsic part of life's cycle. It's not possible to know one without the other.

A glass cannot be half full without also being half empty unless I'm willing to say that it's neither, in which case it's no longer half full or half empty, it just is what it is.

Such is life… eventually.

A Thought to Ponder at Dusk

My imagination is the generator that gives me a sneak preview of my life's next amusement ride.

What will I think of next?

Let tonight's slumber make tomorrow's amusement ride real throughout my day.

A Thought to Ponder at Dawn

The intensity of my focus and intention during my daily prayer, visualization, or meditation practice, helps to expand my consciousness and makes infinite possibilities real.

These manifestations are the tell-tale signs of awakening my sleeping mind.

A Thought to Ponder at Dusk

The moment that I see myself in everyone and everything, I know who I am.

Interestingly enough, no matter how I conduct myself then, is mirroring others.

Note: It is impossible to see in others what I'm not familiar with the inside of my mind.

A Thought to Ponder at Dawn

The awareness of a past thought can only occur in the present moment.

The thought of *love* itself — the full acceptance of both all that is and all that is not — is either created, realized, or remembered in the present moment as well.

When I say that I will love someone or something forever, it can only occur right now and be generated one moment at a time to continue forward.

To feel and express love continuously, it must exist in every breath that I take.

A Thought to Ponder at Dusk

Reflecting on whether or not I currently want to be somewhere other than where I am right now, voids some of the gratitude for the quality of my life and how life works.

Focusing elsewhere also places being present to what's in front of me, far out of reach.

I allow myself to be present to where I am right now and go to sleep with clarity.

A Thought to Ponder at Dawn

Believing in God or not, holds no bearing on the difference that any act of kindness and compassion can make for someone.

Kindness begins and ends with me and as I begin my day, I will look to see where I've been unkind to myself and reconsider holding on to that vantage point.

I can lead with kindness when I choose it for myself.

A Thought to Ponder at Dusk

A mind that sustains a state of realization, understands that what is real, is always *real* and never *true* unless it is referring to the *is-ness* of that particular entity.

The enlightened mind also has the privilege of enjoying freedom, joy, unbridled happiness, and a strong sense of heaven on earth.

With a deep focused intention of daily mindless meditation, I hope to one day *be* the *light* that I already am and not be distracted or reactive.

A Thought to Ponder at Dawn

The words 'belief system', means nothing without placing the 'BS' in their proper places.

As long as my mind continues perceiving anything as real, I and my reality live inside of my 'Belief System' (BS) and not a 'Truth System'(TS).

It's important to realize that I now associate my 'BS' with a *positive* spin because I'm now aware that I've made everything up all along and will begin making up some great BS!

A Thought to Ponder at Dusk

Meet My New Best Friend. PC-WAGS:

Potential - Capacity - Willfulness - Action - Gratitude
Potential is what I'm born with.
Capacity is that which I grow into.
Willfulness is my conscious decision to redirect energy.
Action puts my energy into motion.
Gratitude is what happens when I live an authentic life.
Savoring is giving attention to living presently and enjoying the gift of each moment.

A Thought to Ponder at Dawn

Realizing and acknowledging that 100% of everything that my mind conjures up and thinks is my interpretation.

This is the sacred key of *truthlessness* that unlocks the door to expanded freedom, personal power, and unrecognizable happiness.

Unlocking the door is an incredible accomplishment, walking through it is monumental.

A Thought to Ponder at Dusk

It never matters how silly or paper-thin a fear may be because when it occurs as huge as Mt. Everest, it often evokes anxiety and can be quite debilitating.

Facing fear head-on and embracing it with fortitude and compassion, opens the space for unrecognizable transformation to be realized.

Before gliding into sleep, I set my fears to rest for the evening as well.

A Thought to Ponder at Dawn

Language is a representational method of communication that we use to relate to one another. Despite its many limitations, language conveys individualized perceptions which are often treated concretely.

Sticks and stones might break my bones, but they will heal over time; words, on the other hand, seem to get imprinted into my mind and seem to linger for a lifetime.

What is in my mind's design that appears to in-prison my thoughts permanently?

The answer lies in the Ultimate Failure, which is believing that any part of my reality can ever hold any *truth*.

I humbly recall a genius and master who once said, "Reality is an illusion, albeit a persistent one." - Dr. Albert Einstein.

A Thought to Ponder at Dusk

I will remain strong in my commitment to be authentic and self-expressed because those who matter to me won't mind, and those who do mind, won't matter to me.

Forgiveness, including self-forgiveness, is a great practice, an ideal tool, and a great way of being.

A Thought to Ponder at Dawn

Permanent ownership or possession of anything is impossible to obtain when everything is temporary.

The only possible exception would be energy, which is neither created nor destroyed and always alters its form, but even so, it can't be owned although possibly embodied.

Who I *am* is that energy, called *spirit*, which is neither my mind nor my body.

What would today look like if I were to be mindful of who I am and watch how it influences my reality and my physical body?

A Thought to Ponder at Dusk

I have no control over my reputation — that is for others to decide. My character, however, is based solely on my own influence and participation.

As I fall asleep I inhale my favorite character traits and surrender in my exhale those that I wish to bid a final farewell.

A Thought to Ponder at Dawn

Understanding a person's opinion of me as a direct reflection of their vantage point, allows me to see how I occur to others.

When multiple people share a similar opinion of me, there may be agreement consensus, and commonality, and yet not one of them will match identically or be *true*.

Recognizing how I occur is significant by the power that collective reality holds. Much like in the year 1491, when almost everyone believed that the world was flat, it didn't make it *true*, but it sure made it real in every way that a flat world is perceived.

Believing in the *truth* validates the power of popular consensus, despite the void of the *truth* to begin with. There's nothing to do here but realize this life challenge.

A Thought to Ponder at Dusk

Being able to continually sustain a loving and non-reactive state of mind is at best, Christ-consciousness in action. This is one of the most challenging and important practices in my lifetime.

Any unsettling thoughts or energetic dis-ease which appear tightly bound inside of my mind and body will trigger me to be more mindful in my practice of love and non-reactivity.

Day 133

A Thought to Ponder at Dawn

The outside world seems so very real, yet that which is perceived to be *out there* is only an illusion that is projected from the inside of my mind, which also happens to be a fabricated illusion.

Although all realities are an illusion, the origin of my interpreted reality originates from inside of my mind.

A Thought to Ponder at Dusk

The craving for something to be anything other than what it is at this exact moment gives me a false sense of expectation.

Early childhood is usually loaded with conscious moments of endless wonder, yet as I've grown older, meaningful and significant interpretations have gradually transformed into lighter thoughts, seeming to put them in their proper place.

Part of life's irony is eventually realizing the importance of returning back to creating days of more peaceful moments and infinite wonder.

A Thought to Ponder at Dawn

Although I'm not always aware of being in the present moment, I can't be otherwise.

I will be mindful to wake myself up when I have fallen asleep and strengthen that muscle of awareness so that I may stay awake and enjoy being present in my life.

A wise approach for me is to just assume that I'll be falling asleep sooner or later and to make sure that I have fun when I catch myself or someone else pointing it out.

A Thought to Ponder at Dusk

Learning to honor *time* and *space* is one of the many ways to honor a human existence. A mindset without time or space, however, partially mimics what comes before and after a human life or during breathlessness.

The blissful space in between my exhale and my next inhale mimics breathlessness or a death experience, the only exception being that I will inhale once again.

During mediation, when I focus on that special spacial gap and allow it to intensify, time and space disappear which allows for a sense of nirvana.

Day 135

A Thought to Ponder at Dawn

Although learning how to create good habits is imperative for time-saving efficiency, habitual behavior pulls my mind's focus from remaining present.

I can create a balance of habitual behavior by infusing a Zen mind/beginner's mind into the mix.

For example, I will challenge myself to remain fully aware of everything that I'm doing while driving in my car at the same time that I'm on a Bluetooth call with my cell phone. With practice, an expanding mind should eventually be able to multitask fairly well.

A Thought to Ponder at Dusk

Habitual behavior which is dysfunctional requires a special kind of attention.

The bad habit can only be halted if it is overridden with a new set of thoughts: to first highlight the dysfunctional habit and then create a more empowering one.

Repetition has created the bad habit in the first place and therefore the repetition of good thoughts will eventually create healthy habits in the same manner.

A Thought to Ponder at Dawn

To the naked eye, nothing about a butterfly reveals that it was once a caterpillar — this is an ideal example of transformation.

Transformation can't be forced; it happens and reveals itself in its own time. I can, however, significantly influence my own transformation by choosing the quality of nutrition that my mind and body ingest.

Solid nutrition leads to sound transformation while poor nutrition brings potluck.

Mindfulness is a key component in the process of transformation.

A Thought to Ponder at Dusk

When I'm grateful, I find that my circumstance tends to shift on their own.

When I am grateful, my perspective also expands unexpectedly.

My gratitude mirrors an allowance and acceptance of what is so.

Instead of counting sheep, I will think of everything that I'm grateful for and not bother to count that which is impossible.

A Thought to Ponder at Dawn

A thought directs my focus and intention onto someone or something and carries energy which usually causes a physical manifestation to appear.

Being responsible for my thoughts is a simple concept to understand and yet not always easy to achieve.

Nothing worthwhile is easy or everyone would have attained it and not be taking this challenge on.

The quality of my life depends on me being responsible for the reality that I create.

A Thought to Ponder at Dusk

When consciousness is aware of itself, there is nowhere to go and nothing to do, only here to be — deep meditation brings comfort to this awareness.

With devotional practice, expanded awareness shows up in my daily life.

A Thought to Ponder at Dawn

Being fully present to an experience without having any thought about it, is as close to the *truth* as I will ever have in human reality.

Once a thought about an experience enters my mind, the *truth* vanishes and the reality of it takes over.

A Thought to Ponder at Dusk

The quote, 'the *truth* will set you free' (referring to *absolute,* not relative *truth*), causes separation, division, and war, and is one of the biggest lies humanity has ever told itself or bought into.

Awakening to the concept of the *truth* being as fictitious as reality itself is the only opportunity there is to have peace on earth in any human life.

A Thought to Ponder at Dawn

My interpretations are influenced by my reality and give rise to a day of my own design.

Only I can claim responsibility and hold myself accountable for the impact that my own intentions have.

This is a great thing because it keeps my center of power right where it belongs, within me.

A Thought to Ponder at Dusk

My Belief System is a result of belief systems from people who once lived; I inherited them and continued to adopt others.

Recognizing any unkind or unhealthy beliefs is the perfect opportunity to either do nothing and allow them to continue or alter them by holding a space for them to heal.

Creating new beliefs may be unfamiliar at first and with practice is both possible and probable.

A Thought to Ponder at Dawn

Just as a fish is blind to the water that it swims in, I too am unaware of the 50-70K thoughts that I have daily.

Realizing that I can't even recall having 1000 thoughts per day encourages me to be more mindful of recognizing more of my thoughts.

These staggering numbers are incentive enough to deeply explore my mind space.

A Thought to Ponder at Dusk

Communication is a vehicle for sharing an interpretation and imperfectly expresses the purity of an experience that the mind perceives.

An *experience* itself is pure in nature because it is the *is-ness* of something; it is also the closest to what we call, the *truth*.

Our mind's way of dealing with the *is-ness* of an experience is to make stuff up about it which instantly covers up the *truth* by making it real.

Every mind makes stuff up all the time to relate to and share how we view the pure 'is-ness' of an experience. The limitations of language and my individual mind's limited perspective will always compromise the purity of an experience. I humbly recognize my and everyone's limitations.

A Thought to Ponder at Dawn

When I allow and accept that which is in the space to exist *as it is* and remove my interpretation, instantaneous transformation occurs without any help from my mind.

This awareness opens the space for me to create a new interpretation that better suits me.

I must be mindful of all of my interpretations and monitor them when they become obsolete and no longer serve me.

This is an example of me holding onto my center of power.

A Thought to Ponder at Dusk

My reality is created inside of the only mind I've come to know. No functioning mind can be without one.

The question that I ask is: Do I *have* my reality or does my reality *have* me? When I've lost my power and ability to express myself, I'm at the *effect* of my reality.

Taking full responsibility for my mind's perceptions and interpretations repositions me to be at the *cause* of my reality.

A Thought to Ponder at Dawn

My will, my drive, and my stamina allowed me to see and explore the illusions in my subconscious that I hold as *true*.

This sets the stage for transformation to occur, strengthening my sense of self.

I am blessed to explore a more expanded perspective while holding courage close by when any fears appear.

A Thought to Ponder at Dusk

Sustainable happiness isn't felt when I have more material things or am in a better situation than the one that I'm currently in.

When it is authentic, sustainable happiness is generated from within by *allowing* myself to be right where I am and *accepting* my circumstances as they are.

This allows my state of happiness to flow continually.

I, therefore, set my sights on allowing and accepting people, places, and things to be as they are.

A Thought to Ponder at Dawn

The Law of Impermanence is a process that is out of our control; this law also confirms that everything has a beginning, a middle, and an end.

The times when I embrace and go with the flow of life, I am free.

The moment that I resist that which I have no control over, there is upset, and difficulty, and I am owned by whatever it is.

The challenge is to recognize my resistance quickly enough to surrender and just ride the wave of freedom.

A Thought to Ponder at Dusk

The color and vividness of painted brush strokes that my creative perspectives transfer onto the canvas of my reality are directly proportional to how I see the world.

No matter who I might be influenced or inspired by, it is my hand that strokes the brush.

Taking both the blame and credit as mine without threatening my sense of self-worth is my badge of empowerment.

A Thought to Ponder at Dawn

There is a place called nowhere, where nothing exists, and everything is possible.

It's a sacred realm where consciousness remains undifferentiated and the playground for unbridled freedom and joy can easily be realized.

Like a secret passageway that's located inside of my mind, it opens when I am still, quiet, and all thoughts have flown through it long enough until there are no thoughts left to think; I can enter and just be.

I recognize that nowhere and everywhere are one — and that's home to my spirit.

A Thought to Ponder at Dusk

The University of Greater Consciousness, which is not found in any collegiate brick and mortar dwelling, offers a special diploma — a humbled doctorate in Spiritual Wisdom.

Much like where the Kingdom of God resides, this *gift* of this wisdom comes from awakening inside of me. Worldly knowledge, on the other hand, comes from outside sources and is packaged inside of a collection of past interpretations.

Both areas of learning deserve equal time because the children who learn to meditate early on and look within live healthier and happier lives.

A Thought to Ponder at Dawn

Knowledge is to my Mind, what Wisdom is to my Individual Consciousness.

The sources are completely different, and it is in my realm of jurisdiction to create the perfect blending of these realities.

I take on the lifetime role of custodian of my reality and do my best to navigate without blame.

A Thought to Ponder at Dusk

In the collective consciousness, I've agreed that who I am, is whom I and others think I am.

This is an inaccurate approach to living an expansive life because it separates me from knowing my authentic self as the individual consciousness — *spirit* — within.

Meditation practice, daily prayers, and moments to refocus on greater awareness, allows me to tip the scales back to balance for me to gain a more holistic perspective on my human experience.

A Thought to Ponder at Dawn

When I'm awake, I am clear that I am neither my mind nor my body. The process of self-realization is both a great gift and a lifelong challenge.

The longer I remain awake, the more I'm present to the authenticity of love itself.

I look forward to the day that I'm comfortable being consistently in life's flow without a paddle.

A Thought to Ponder at Dusk

Being engaged, non-reactive, and remaining indifferent, are all key characteristics of a self-realized individual.

Holding no distinction between that which is positive and negative, while living in an illusion of duality (yin and yang), is a key attribute of an enlightened soul.

A Thought to Ponder at Dawn

A shift from *knowing* about something into actually *being* it occurs when I'm aware of it, allow, accept it, and do nothing to alter or force it to occur.

Seeing it brings visible clarity while allowing and accepting it, enables me to be present as a witness and be part of the transformational process.

No matter what the challenge, the process of transformation occurs when I surrender to it, take it out of my hands, and do nothing to help it along.

A Thought to Ponder at Dusk

With keen focus and intention, I create the powerful energy that is required for any form of manifestation to occur.

By placing my focus and intention on *peace* and *calm* in this moment and over the next 10 - 15 minutes, I allow my mind to take me somewhere in space without time.

A Thought to Ponder at Dawn

Retrieving my power center is oftentimes a result of embracing *gratitude* and understanding the greater higher order of things.

Trusting in this process allows what is both good and not so good, to blanket fear with hope and brings about a new reality with a sense of renewed empowerment.

Add to that the awareness of life's temporality and my reality is immensely freeing.

A Thought to Ponder at Dusk

To fear any inevitable, the greatest of all which is death kills off the possibility of life being fully embraced and lived.

I ask the Universe, "if I am to leave tonight, to please take me in while asleep."

Otherwise, I demand to be rid of all fears of anything inevitable as well as anything I have no control over.

I delve into tonight's sleep with an open heart and restful mind.

A Thought to Ponder at Dawn

My mind is an *Insistent Interpreter*, wired to fabricate interpretations by assessing, evaluating, judging, and then providing meaning and significance to things, whether or not they are valuable.

My mind's awakened conscience, also known as the *Gate Keeper*, can either move my mind's monologs into dialogues by speaking thoughts into existence, or it can decide to keep my lips sealed until those internal thoughts disappear on their own.

The focused practice of *gatekeeping* is key to greater more powerful communication.

A Thought to Ponder at Dusk

It's a mistake to think that sharing any interpretation about an experience, is the same thing as sharing the experience itself... it is not.

An experience is the *isness* or the *essence* of something pure, in and of itself, and void of any meaning.

Using my free will, I create interpretations of my experiences that bring meaning and significance to them.

This process creates my reality whether I choose to be responsible for it or not. Being fully accountable keeps my power core in place and my life powerful.

A Thought to Ponder at Dawn

An experience is instantly stripped from its pure state and thrown into the sea of reality whenever the mind conjures up an interpretation.

This is the preferred manner in which we relate to an experience. My interpreted perceptions block the pureness allowing me to live in a world of illusion inside of my mind.

One way for me to regain a sense of truth, however, is through meditation the moment when I become mindless.

A Thought to Ponder at Dusk

Living my life from past interpretations rolls over many of the old segments into current thinking which in turn, gives way to a predictable future.

By understanding that I've both inherited and either created and/or adopted a particular vantage point, I recognize that I'm sourcing my entire reality. Altering my thinking is only the first step in creating a new reality that excites me.

The second step is creating a practice to keep a new view alive by taking action and being conscious to refresh my thoughts throughout the day and every day. This strengthens and stabilizes my new perspective in an always-changing world that only exists inside of my mind.

A Thought to Ponder at Dawn

The words *truth* and reality, their respective meaning, and how we relate to them, live inside of our minds and last for as long as we choose to relate to them in the same manner.

Before and after the creation of any meaning given to something for that matter, the is-ness or essence of what that something is, still *is* what it is. It is my human interpretation that turns the *is-ness* of things into a temporary reality and existence.

A Thought to Ponder at Dusk

Animals have survival methods that allow them to live in the wild. We, on the other hand, have fabricated sophisticated survival methods — we learned how to prey upon one another to gain power and dominion.

The creation of currency, kingdoms, governments, and taxes, along with laws that govern property and land ownership, has crippled our natural God-given existence, and challenged our access to authentic freedom and survival. The dysfunctional illusion of choosing order over fellowship, compassion, kindness, and love, has been one of the greatest mistakes of our existence.

John Lennon once said, "Imagine all the people, living life in peace..." This concept will remain in our imagination as long as we remain paralyzed in thought. The silver lining is to see this and choose another reality that feeds and nourishes my soul and allows me to imagine and dream.

A Thought to Ponder at Dawn

We possess the potential for universal love and greatness, yet for this kind of monumental shift to be realized, we must all activate our willful capacity to be *love-in-action*. The current predictable course is for self-annihilation and underscores the importance of our focus to be on dealing more kindly and lovingly with one another.

Carl Sagan once shared with us that all the life we have ever known has come as a result of living on a tiny blue dot in the cosmic doc, called earth, and no one from outer space is going to come to save us from ourselves… it is up to us… it is up to me.

A Thought to Ponder at Dusk

With each mind awakening, the number of mindful light workers may only increase by one, but each one can touch countless lives.

In our childhood dreams, some of us were once able to fly, while others had achievements that only were made possible by imagination.

Should I awaken tomorrow morning, I believe it's time to think like Walt Disney.

A Thought to Ponder at Dawn

Whether or not our extinction comes before or during our planet's unavoidable end, our solar system, like all others, will perish nonetheless and be reabsorbed into the cosmos.

With my limited time here I hope to make a significant difference for others, especially those who matter most to me.

Each morning I create good intentions to positively impact others while knowing in my heart that my life will have mattered after I'm gone.

A Thought to Ponder at Dusk

The wisdom of an enlightened mind knows of the sea of infinite reality from which limitless perspectives can be newly chosen and adopted at any moment in time.

It's up to me to finally stop thinking that my reality or any other reality for that matter is *true* so that I can choose a more appropriate one that upgrades the quality of my life.

When I examine the thoughts which are dysfunctional and need to be pitched, I'm able to cherish the ones to keep while seeking out ones that inspire me.

A Thought to Ponder at Dawn

Astrophysicists have scientifically discovered and proven that the universe is expanding.

This is a brilliant finding from created perspectives that exist in a collective reality.

It's mindful for advanced thinkers to err on the side of continuous discovery, rather than give concrete or meaningful significance to any reality simply by its findings.

The reason for this is that given enough time, everything changes anyhow.

Flexibility is key in going with the flow and is also the path of least resistance.

A Thought to Ponder at Dusk

Being mindful of allowing my reality to continuously expand, requires that my perspective of wonder and exploration override what I discover. Although I will gain some pretty significant factual knowledge, I must remember that 'Wisdom, is knowing that I don't know'.

It's time to quiet myself down, breathe softly into sleep, and tap into all that's possible.

A Thought to Ponder at Dawn

The more people that believe and agree with my reality, the more successful I'll become. The proof of this is seen in the work of Jesus, Mother Theresa, Gandhi, Martin Luther King, Hitler, Osama bin Ladin, Castro, Bill Gates, Mark Zuckerberg, and any other powerful leader.

Given the existing challenges in the world, it is essential to upgrade my beliefs. This mindset is more in line with a healthier community that better supports humanity. Although chances are having *peace on earth* is improbable, I'd like to stand with every Miss America on this one and live with this in mind regardless.

A Thought to Ponder at Dusk

At times I've had a false sense that my mind has limitations when in fact the possibilities of reality are infinite.

When I silence my mind, access to *all that is* appears, and I feel renewed.

I close my eyes, and take slow, easy breaths, opening my mind to all that is possible.

A Thought to Ponder at Dawn

The way to have a challenge resolve itself for good is to meet it head-on by embracing it and never going around it.

This means that I allow it, accept it as it is, and then watch it disappear in its own time.

Realizing that this is how transformation works, helps refocus my thoughts on things that nourish and bring me joy.

Today I look at what joy and empowerment I can bring to others.

A Thought to Ponder at Dusk

During the undisclosed limited number of days that I have left in my life, my interpretations and actions will continue to determine the quality of my life.

Tonight I will either drift off with a clear conscience, need to cleanse my thoughts with self-forgiveness to create a clean space or leave things unfinished.

I'll only be able to create a new day of my own design if my conscience is clear.

A Thought to Ponder at Dawn

When I let go of thinking about how life *should* be and what it *should* look like, I can find joy and peace in the autobiography that I currently continue to write and live.

Gratitude does go a long way and happens when I stop *shoulding* all over myself.

A Thought to Ponder at Dusk

What would be available if, for the rest of my life, I removed all *truth* from my reality, allowing my feelings and emotions to just be the reactive responses to the thoughts that live inside of my head?

One thing which comes to mind is a greater sense of freedom along with a whole lot more options to choose from.

A Thought to Ponder at Dawn

Being mindful allows objectivity to be a part of my feelings and emotions and effectively gauges what goes on inside of my reality.

The greater the clarity, the more authentic and mature are my feelings and emotions.

When I find myself being reactive to others and circumstances, it's important to realize that I am neither my feelings nor my emotions.

This gives me the advantage to deal with challenges with greater ease and logic, and not being so quick to act irresponsibly.

A Thought to Ponder at Dusk

One of the finest illustrations of a mind's brilliance is its realization that everything inside of its reality, including its identity, is generated by forms of ever-changing thought.

The stream of life that flows, opens up the possibility of a realm far beyond both the mind's reality and identity. Having a sustainable awareness of neutrality and indifference is *a new way of being* and can allow me to be my own Buddha.

A Thought to Ponder at Dawn

Without having my mind intact, people, places, and things would have little if no meaning and nothing would exist, including the very concepts of what *nothing* and *everything* is.

It is because of my mind and identity that I have an illusion of human life.

Thought energy that enters into it from outside, along with the thought energy that I muster up inside, is translated through the limitations of what my mind can wrap itself around to understand and then attempt to share. Being aware of this vantage point is both humbling and gratifying at the same time.

A Thought to Ponder at Dusk

I have a sense of profound intimacy when someone understands me (my mind). The subject matter discussed is what determines the quality of a relationship that is formed.

When multiple people understand my thinking, a sense of community is created. When there's little or no understanding, I'm allowed to either open my heart to authentic self-love and love others just the same or feel lost and alone. The determining factor is whether or not I know who and what I am.

A Thought to Ponder at Dawn

Normal perceptivity confirms that there's an out there, yet there is no *out there*. All thoughts about my life, everyone, and everything around me are created and live inside of my mind.

Knowing this, I still default to believing this crazy thought that there's an *out there*.

To place all the responsibility and accountability on me for my interpretation of the world that I see and live in, I must once and for all own that the *out there* is always inside my mind, period.

What lies behind my eyes is the generator of my reality and my world.

A Thought to Ponder at Dusk

Chances are that today, I continue to remain a product of my yesterday's choices.

What might I choose right now to reinterpret my perspective, such that I can create an authentic shift in now-moments so that tomorrow's now-moments would be worth living into?

I will contemplate this quite seriously because the quality of my life depends upon it.

A Thought to Ponder at Dawn

The impact of knowing that my autobiography is nothing more than an amazing novel filled with an array of fictional chapters provides the freedom to create and enjoy any reality that I so choose.

I will use the act of brushing my teeth every morning to trigger a reminder to create a day of my own design.

I will also use showering at night as another trigger to release all the day's energy so that I may cleanse and clear my mind and body for a restful night's sleep.

A Thought to Ponder at Dusk

Young children often live, play, and are happy, sad, and present in each moment. As an adult, however, living inside the concept of time and space, I'm often challenged to stay on task or on schedule which as a result, often manifests stress in my day.

Until it's habitual, I will put reminders in place that inspire me to enjoy healthier nutrition and exercise protocol as well as get better rest.

Regular massages, devotional meditation, and the practice of prayer will not only help to clear my mind, which is essential to removing stress, but it will also help me to sleep better.

A Thought to Ponder at Dawn

Climbing the proverbial ladder to the top is a powerful and motivational concept that reinforces the illusion of never being fully satisfied with being right where I am or during each step of my climb.

This is based on the *assumption* that there's someplace better to arrive at than right here.

Realizing that the ladder is my ladder, helps make the climb, my climb and no one else.

I powerfully create my climb and make sure to have fun at each rung I step on to.

A Thought to Ponder at Dusk

My mind is notoriously stupid when it relentlessly tries to keep my identity, my reality, and my surroundings stabilized, and in place and life status quo, in a world that is constantly changing.

As I release and say goodbye to this day, I open my heart and mind to the vastness and temporality of the consciousness which flows in the world of sleep.

I will look into the darkness when my eyes are closed and find the light.

A Thought to Ponder at Dawn

My mind functions tirelessly, non-stop, and often effortlessly, to evaluate, assess, and judge, to create beliefs about things.

Until and after I begin to live daily in an awakened state of non-reactivity and indifference, I will practice visualizations and meditations to support sustenance.

Until that occurs, I recognize these beliefs are as temporary and transient as life itself.

A Thought to Ponder at Dusk

From birth until death, my mind is my pilot and my gut is my co-pilot. I commit my mind to a lifetime of service to myself as well as to others, by being responsible to keep it open, refreshed, and inspirational.

The quality of nutrition that I allow to enter my gut illustrates the level of respect that I hold for the body's internal awesome intelligence.

A Thought to Ponder at Dawn

An enlightened mind has learned the difference between needing to figure things out and seeking to understand, without the burden of being driven by wants, needs, and desires.

Enlightenment is not a place to get to nor is it a finish line.

It is a conscious stand that I take to co-pilot my life with the divine.

The more awakened I am, the more I am grateful and forgiving, and the greater I can love.

I challenge myself to think of the people, places, and things which still upset me so that I can see where I will place today's focus.

A Thought to Ponder at Dusk

The enlightened mind is at peace and takes comfort in living within the illusion of reality while realizing that at any moment, there can be a significant shift in perspective.

Expanding individual consciousness, however, is possible when I remain calm and non-reactionary. Doing so allows me to continue having fun and play within the reality that I've created.

A Thought to Ponder at Dawn

The specific indicator that my mind has yet to be awakened is recognizing that my future remains quite predictable.

It is when I can live comfortably and thrive inside of uncertainty, that I am free and filled with possibility.

Taking this consciously into my day can surely allow me to create a very different day.

A Thought to Ponder at Dusk

When I'm aware of being in the moment, I'm still inside of my mind about it.

When I recognize that I'm in the moment, I'm both in and out of my mind.

When a moment and I are one, however, that's when I'm out of my mind.

The most obvious way of achieving a state of being in the moment, aside from death, is when entering into a deep meditation — this is a state of mindlessness.

A Thought to Ponder at Dawn

Believing what I'm conceiving makes achieving possible.

These are key steps in the genesis of my creations.

Next, assimilation is a direct result of actions that I take.

The quality of implementation is based on the intensity of my focused intention.

I promise to be laser-focused on my daily intention and evaluate at night.

A Thought to Ponder at Dusk

I will no longer hold myself as a victim of circumstance, my emotions, or feelings.

I seek to use them, embrace them, and have dominion over them in addition to disallowing them from obstructing the flow of my life.

Emotions and feelings are prime indicators of where I am and allow me to see what still has yet to be transformed and bring peace.

I release any lingering negative feelings and emotions and slip into regenerative slumber.

A Thought to Ponder at Dawn

Having a backbone allows me to stand on my own two feet.

Having a wishbone is for dreams not yet realized, while a funny bone is for me to take life more joyfully.

Whenever I find that I have a bone to pick with someone, I will remember that I have more than enough bones of my own thank you.

A Thought to Ponder at Dusk

Every moment contains bliss and freedom when I'm in the *now* of it.

When I'm present in each moment, there is no relative opposite.

Inside every *now* moment lies creation itself.

As I close my eyes and continually clear the space for what lies ahead, I'm able to drift into that *now* space more easily — there is peace.

A Thought to Ponder at Dawn

Happiness and freedom are a direct reflection of my thoughts.

Whenever a thought comes into mind, that's my golden opportunity to show myself my strength by managing each thought the way I'd like them to play out.

When I'm aware, I am the *Gate Keeper* of thoughts and have the power to police any unwelcome thoughts and encourage and nourish those which are worth my while.

A Thought to Ponder at Dusk

Embracing my identity as a harbor of playfulness, insignificance, and kindness, helps to exonerate my spirit from a captivating mind.

Children oftentimes derive freedom and happiness through fantasy and imagination. As adults, we generate freedom and happiness in the same manner but need to coin it differently so that it appears more mature.

We, therefore, call it creativity and inspiration. Any life worth living is generated in fantasy land through a realm of imagination, which is the same place that generates a life of turmoil and sadness.

Understanding this seriously motivates me to choose my creations wisely.

Day 169

A Thought to Ponder at Dawn

Whenever an enlightened mind's perspective makes an interpretation that creates a reality about a person, place, or thing, it takes full ownership over whatever it then perceives as real.

This is because it knows that everything on the outside is merely a mirror of what is on the inside; it's always an *inside job*.

When I'm upset or challenged, I do my best to return quickly to this awareness and not fix anything, but rather realize what caused the loss of power.

I can then rethink my thoughts by creating a new interpretation to live by.

A Thought to Ponder at Dusk

A powerful mind is both responsible and accountable for everything that it creates because it knows who created it.

I look back on today as a learning experience and see where I've given up my power and where I could have done things differently.

This is a perfect opportunity for me to gain greater understanding and be grateful for this wisdom.

A Thought to Ponder at Dawn

The enlightened mind dances in neutrality without a need to fix anything while quietly embracing peace.

Today I seek to remain non-reactive to all people and situations throughout my day. I intend to be playful and light with this, especially in the face of adversity and plan to give myself a grade of pass/ fail by day's end. This is a 'to-me, from-me' gift, which I intend to have fun with, in addition to taking this on with serious intention.

A Thought to Ponder at Dusk

Three key rules to never receive any kind of criticism:

RULE 1. Do Nothing.
RULE 2. Say Nothing.
RULE 3. Be Nothing.

I would rather choose to welcome all assessments, evaluations, and judgments and can hold them as benign in their impact as long as I maintain my power center. Although I might initially feel uneasy at first, I promise to receive all feedback as well-intended attempts by others to make their contribution.

I will surely be mindful that when it's my turn to contribute to others, I'll be sensitive enough that they too may see my contribution with good intention.

A Thought to Ponder at Dawn

The question I ask myself is, "What kind of world will I choose to create and live in today when there are so many real worlds to choose from?"

I must be mindful to realize that whatever world I do choose to see *out there*, exists solely inside of my mind anyhow.

Until enlightenment is at my doorstep, I will probably slip focus countless times throughout my day about who's been in charge all along — little 'ol me!

A Thought to Ponder at Dusk

My brain uses my body's sensory organs to retrieve information from the outside. My mind translates this data and creates assessments of what it perceives on the outside.

An enlightened mind is not tricked by any illusion of what we call, *out there*, and instead turns to introspection and assessment. Whatever is *out there* is, and whatever *out there* means, it simply *is* what it is.

The meaning of having an *out there* reinforces that particular illusion.

Understanding that reality itself is illusory, I can create whatever illusions I want now. This places my center of power where it belongs… somewhere inside of the illusion of me.

A Thought to Ponder at Dawn

An Important Reflection:

I am the teacher of what I have lived, an artisan of the life that I currently live, and an inspired novice in the projected life that I'm living into.

The life that I live may be an inspiration to others just as theirs may be to mine. Imagining and creating any expression of me requires my focus and attention. I am grateful for the life I have because it's the only one I'll ever know.

A Thought to Ponder at Dusk

What would reality be like if my brain didn't supply my mind with sensory data?

Before the moment that Helen Keller learned sign language, there was no way for her to interpret any of the stimuli that her brain was experiencing. Once she learned how to communicate through sign language, she shared that her life seemed like a damp plot of earth, while before then, she hadn't the words for it.

From that moment, Helen's reality was able to grow and expand. My mind does its best to assimilate my brain's limited data to create an interpretation for me to understand and share.

A Thought to Ponder at Dawn

An enlightened mind dances playfully in neutrality and is void of needing to fix anything.

When fully present I am a spectator of a magnificent human life. When I'm able to sustain this, I'll be given the choice to live my life in a manner that is no longer common or usual and feel blessed to create a new way. Optimally, choosing how to create my life is merely a matter of balance.

A Thought to Ponder at Dusk

Dying to leave my earth suit is as much of an illusion as living inside of it is. When I stop engaging with death and the mourning process in the usual manner, I'll have the ability to listen to loved ones who have already left their body.

This is how it works:

a. I find a quiet place to get real still.
b. I think of a loved one who's transitioned and ask them a question.
c. I then listen closely to the monologue inside of my head.

A moment occurs when I'll hear things that I would have never thought to think. I may even hear their voice just as I remembered it, speaking inside of my head. By listening until there is total silence, I will know that they are done. Having conversations with God or loved ones is possible for everyone. By writing this in a journal in real-time instead, I'll be able to see my mind stop thinking and where I begin taking dictation.

A Thought to Ponder at Dawn

When I witness my own consciousness, I can see its purity and its challenges.

My challenge is not to take it personally but engage like a loving parent and minister with good intentions and be the best custodian a consciousness could ever have.

I am with my thoughts every moment of my life and yet, I'm unaware of the tens of thousands of thoughts I have.

By making it a priority and practicing to witness as many thoughts as I can throughout the day, I will begin to uncover and learn much more about myself.

A Thought to Ponder at Dusk

Each moment is separate in and of itself and yet, belongs to the stream of past and infinite moments yet to be.

Not all of life's streaming moments are healthy, especially when there is pain, heartache, discomfort, and dis-ease. At any time, I can redirect my stream of real moments onto another stream. Practice and repetition are key in bringing sustainability to whatever I choose to focus on.

It's a great challenge and gift to realize that I'm the captain of my streaming.

Day 175

A Thought to Ponder at Dawn

When the mind and body receive optimal nourishment, health is a natural state of balance.

Dis-ease is the natural state of imbalance caused by overindulgence of disrespectful thoughts and actions which sabotage and dishonor the beauty of my spirit.

I commit to being conscious of where I sabotage my mind and body and uncover the **B**elief **S**ystem which supports this behavior.

A Thought to Ponder at Dusk

When I completely stop what I'm doing, do nothing, and witness everything around me, I'm able to see life's beautiful flow of energy.

That's an ideal moment when I realize that nothing ever stays the same and everything is always authentically new.

Doing this throughout my day, every couple of hours and for only a minute, can bring a sense of peace worth having.

A Thought to Ponder at Dawn

Unlike my mind and body, which will eventually expire, I am an eternal expression of infinite consciousness and have all of the time in the universe in which to be.

As the *spirit of light,* what can I do for my mind and body in this short bleep of eternity, to have the chance to embrace the magnificence of earthly life?

I imprint this question in my mind and will live my life from it.

A Thought to Ponder at Dusk

The past provides a chronological understanding of how old thoughts continuously influence present moments and illustrates transparency for a predictable future.

Being aware that I hold the wand which alters anything and everything, I have the power needed to intervene in the old process and influence my present moments for a new and predictable future.

A Thought to Ponder at Dawn

Realizing that I'm the sole creator of my own reality, may just help curb or put a stop to many of the excess life challenges I face.

There are also unavoidable challenges to which I can still fall victim and admitting that I perceive life challenges as life challenges, I then have the power to redefine them as life opportunities because life simply *is what* it is and I have the final say.

This realization is paramount because it underscores that I am the creator of my reality. I set my intention to create what I wish to see occur and then humbly accept what comes.

A Thought to Ponder at Dusk

When receiving intuitive information, I am mindful of the limited data being collected by my brain and my mind's own challenged capacity to interpret an experience.

Many spiritual leaders make this mistake when they write a book and although it's not their intention, the reader is not forewarned about it not being pure and therefore, *true*. It's important to remember that sharing the information that is collected in this manner is real, valid, significant, and often remains meaningful enough to contribute.

A Thought to Ponder at Dawn

Monty Python's movie, 'The Meaning of Life,' clearly illustrates how our reality can easily inject an abundance of significance, silliness, and creatively warped perspectives into our life.

The movie is brilliant, funny, and worth the watch if you've not seen it, and if you have, it may be a great time to watch it again with a new pair of eyes.

A most extraordinary insight which I embrace daily is knowing that the only meaning of life that I have, is the meaning that I give to it.

I create a day of special awareness, where every interpretation that I make is mine alone.

A Thought to Ponder at Dusk

Enlightenment is possible the moment I realize that everything is made up in my mind.

What follows is a lifetime of keeping the lights on, remaining awake, and knowing that giving my power away causes upset and holding firm to my core, brings me joy.

This is my playing field for a greater and more fulfilling consciousness and therefore I breathe in all that is possible and exhale old beliefs which do not serve me.

A Thought to Ponder at Dawn

Sentiments of *truth* evaporate from reality when mindfulness of a greater consciousness appears and encourages a new and preferential comfort zone of inquiry, wonder, imagination, indifference, detachment, and the ability to not be reactive.

Daily meditation practice is my doorway to abundant joy and a sense of sustainable inner freedom.

Whether I'm a novice or a devoted yogi, infinite expansion of consciousness awaits.

A Thought to Ponder at Dusk

A secret to living mindfully is to allow myself to be exactly where I am and whole-hearty accept where I am as well.

This grants me the opportunity to realize that *I am where I am* and the awareness to explore all the interpretations and meanings that I've fabricated and still hold onto which no longer serve me.

A Thought to Ponder at Dawn

Whom I think I am and what I believe is real, gives me the vantage point from which I view everything in my life. Like a projector casts its film onto a movie screen, so too does my mind project its interpretations onto a canvas called the *outside world*. The origin of all reflections of reality is generated from a projector called my mind.

To be 100% liable for whatever I see and feel is almost too overwhelming to be with, yet I know that until I do, I'll be owned and shackled by it.

As a responsible producer and director of my own movie, I will be mindful of the reflections which I put out for others to see.

A Thought to Ponder at Dusk

Realizing that my identity *has me* and that I don't quite know what it's like to *have* an identity, places me in a state of not knowing who I am and at the same time, at the threshold of self-realization.

My ultimate failure in my life has been to think that my reality was ever *true*. *Truth* has locked me inside of a reality that otherwise would have been easily changeable.

Once fully in charge of my reality, I will reinvent my life however I so choose.

A Thought to Ponder at Dawn

It's pretty standard that when something needs to be done, we ask a busy person because they tend to be more efficient and productive than those who are not.

Because I've made it to this point in my reading, I acknowledge that inspirational perspectives help motivate me to create a life that I love and can thrive in.

What can I say or do to pay it forward to someone who can use some inspiration?

A Thought to Ponder at Dusk

Much like the rippling effect seen from tossing a small stone into calm water, a slight shift in my perspective can in time, create a radiant change. Desiring quick gratification will often produce a big letdown, yet with patience and understanding, the size of the rippling circles continues to grow significantly over time.

Although immediate results may occur, craving instant change has been one of my greatest challenges whenever I've altered my perspective.

Life will never offer me a timetable guarantee for shifts to occur which is why I sometimes practice inhaling patience during my meditation practice.

A Thought to Ponder at Dawn

When unencumbered by my identity, my mind has access to infinite possibility. The moment I argue for any of my limitations, by my hand, they become mine. Being mindful of what I speak, I'm able to abolish inaccurate, unpleasant, disempowering, jibber-jabber.

I forgive myself whenever I fall asleep, pick myself up, and am mindful once more. I open my heart and welcome this day with an awakened mind.

A Thought to Ponder at Dusk

A miracle is a conceptual placeholder for that which has yet to be scientifically explained. Once data, facts, and figures, are brought to light, evaluated, and assimilated, the reason for why something is the way that it is gets created.

At this moment that particular miracle vanishes, and it becomes a scientific fact. There appears to be no resemblance between a caterpillar and a butterfly and there is.

Looking into the cocoon, modern science has made it possible for us to see the magnificent progression of this transformation. When I'm quiet and present to my mind and body, it mirrors a caterpillar's cocoon and I'm able to see my own metamorphosis taking place.

Looking deeper, I may see a genesis and realize that the kingdom of God is already within me waiting to be realized.

A Thought to Ponder at Dawn

Five Key Steps in witnessing challenging thoughts transform themselves:

1. Meet whatever the challenge is, head-on, and look it square in the eye.
2. Allow my challenge the space it needs to simply remain as it is in that moment.
3. Embrace and accept it in each moment that it's happening.
4. Sit on my hands, observe it, and with closed lips do and say nothing.
5. Finally, knowing that it will transform in its own time, I will refocus my thoughts on something else worth my while and recreate the joy and happiness I intend to have.

A Thought to Ponder at Dusk

Taking personal troubles or those of the world to sleep at night creates dis-ease.

I willfully disallow any unsettling thoughts to infiltrate my cells or alter my physiology. My focus at night begins with decompression and showering away the day's challenges. Rest, rejuvenation, energization, and sleep at bedtime, are essential for my mind and body to get what it needs and ready themselves for a new day.

A Thought to Ponder at Dawn

A significant and meaningful past sculpts my identity and view of my world.

I intend to neutralize any associated energetic charges yet not erase anything. Recognition of my choices and actions are powerful means to responsibly alter things.

Anything that I make up, is as valid as any belief that I've inherited or adopted thus far. With practice and repetition, the transformational shift will occur on its own. I will remember to relate to any sense of failure at this with fun and ease.

A Thought to Ponder at Dusk

Despite what I've heard, it is possible to change someone's behavior. This is accomplished by genuinely altering my behavior.

Just like I can't argue with someone who doesn't want to argue, I will be the change that I wish to see in others and begin to live my life and have it be the lesson I'd wish to teach.

I close my eyes and see that this beautiful shift has already happened and allow it to infiltrate every cell of my body.

Day 185

A Thought to Ponder at Dawn

When I genuinely love someone, there is no desire to change them, only to support them as they transform. I accept and allow others to be as they are and reveal their greatness.

When this wisdom permeates into every cell in my body, I will come to know *heaven on earth* as a new standard way of living.

In place of this being just a nice passage, I promise myself to be present to how my love of others causes me to observe and not intervene in someone else's path.

I'm smiling because I know that this passage has not been read in vain.

A Thought to Ponder at Dusk

Being loved and cherished by someone is quite satisfying and nourishing, however deeply loving someone opens my heart to unbridled happiness and is the gift of a lifetime.

I will close my eyes and think of five people whom I love dearly and embrace them with joy as I take them with me into my dreams.

A Thought to Ponder at Dawn

When going from my bed to the bathroom occurs like scaling Mt. Everest, it becomes crystal clear that I've not honored my body. My body is a sacred temple; I only have one and it can't be traded in for a newer model.

I faithfully consider a new lifetime choice for healthier living.

This includes good nutrition for better fuel energy, exercise for an optimal physique, and mind exercises for healthier thoughts.

I seriously and playfully take this on because the quality of my life depends upon it.

A Thought to Ponder at Dusk

When my mind becomes aware of being in the moment, in that particular moment, it is no longer in that moment; instead, my mind is having thoughts about being in that moment.

Whenever I'm in the moment, my mind is sometimes thoughtless, yet laser focused. I can cleanse my mind and clear out my thoughts by focusing on my breath. Focusing on my next 20 inhales and exhales will allow me to be present. Done correctly, I will experience something unique after the 20th exhale. Focusing on my breath will begin to calm my mind and rejuvenate my body.

A Thought to Ponder at Dawn

A possible driving force behind conditional love is an underlying desire to have an agreement of mutual care with someone.

This is also a possible underlying craving that lays the foundation for an unhealthy tone and culture in the relationship.

The power vibration behind unconditional love, however, is an unwavering ability to *stand* in love with someone and not give my power away by *falling* in love.

The irony about both kinds of love is that they often appear in reality simultaneously.

The challenge is finding the sweet spot of harmony and balance.

A Thought to Ponder at Dusk

My identity can thrive inside of my reality when I allow *me* (*spirit*) to illuminate my mind into an awakened state.

This allows me to see reality as the illusion that it is.

I close my eyes at night and see only *me* and the *light* that *I AM*.

A Thought to Ponder at Dawn

Transformation of any vantage point always occurs in the present and is a result of a sudden jolt of clarity and understanding.

Remaining conscious in this state of mind is as simple as it is to understand as it is challenging to achieve.

This magnificent portal to enlightenment is mine to embrace and depends on how driven and committed I am to watching it occur.

A Thought to Ponder at Dusk

Thoughts come to mind from an infinite sea of thoughts called, the *thoughtmosphere.*

With practice, I become aware of multiple thoughts occurring simultaneously. Eventually, I'm able to sense thought energy just before the thought is created.

My level of sensitivity to energy is dependent upon how well I honor my physical, mental, and emotional health — the cleaner my mind, the clearer my perceptions.

This is a simple 'cause and effect' equation — garbage in, garbage out. As I fall asleep tonight I focus on cleansing and clarity for a brighter awakened state.

Day 189

A Thought to Ponder at Dawn

Thinking that my mind is limited in its current capacity is quite humbling.

Realizing that my mind is expanding continually and is limitless, is even more humbling.

Even a genius' mind can be humbled when realizing how much it still doesn't know.

I acknowledge that no one is below or above me and realize that my mind's spiritual, emotional, and intellectual capacity at birth, remains an essential gift for me to even have a reality. Any form of mind expansion remains my responsibility.

A Thought to Ponder at Dusk

Whether or not I agree that I am an eternal spirit, has no bearing on my eternal existence.

We all receive the privilege of enlightenment eventually; mindfulness either comes at the doorway to our transition or during our life as human beings.

At the point of realization, I understand that I am an eternal being vibrating inside of a human experience and my mind finally knows that I am that *I Am*.

A Thought to Ponder at Dawn

Make no mistake and my life remains small. Fail with grace and open arms of lightheartedness and I hold a master key to filling my life with happiness and freedom.

What challenges will I face today that will bring gratitude and accomplishment?

A Thought to Ponder at Dusk

Being in control or having ownership in anything are two of the silliest, made-up beliefs that mankind has ever masterminded for itself. Simply speaking, these beliefs reinforce why we are the only species on the planet who has ever had to pay money to live here.

Along with governmental power of every kind, the creation of currency has stripped us of our human right to live freely and in an unencumbered state.

Until I free myself *within* the confines of the prison cell of my reality, whether I agree with it or not, I will be affected by the belief that 'He who dies with the most toys wins.'

My access to freedom and center of power is only a mind shift away.

A Thought to Ponder at Dawn

I do my best to take in and consume enough of everything to have a healthy life.

When I over-indulge, like it or not, I'm still accountable for any dis-ease created inside of my mind and body.

Although I assume this is about nutritional consumption, I am mindful to keep my life balanced at home, at work, at play, and inside of my mind itself, as often as I can. Anytime I overdo it or take in too much of life's drama, the homeostasis is gone.

Being in charge of monitoring my equilibrium is simply to understand yet not easy to do.

A Thought to Ponder at Dusk

In deep meditation, the silence found in the gap between thoughts is indivisible, unrecognizable, and beyond blissful because it exists outside of the realm of time and space.

In addition, the space between an exhale and my next inhale mirrors what it will be like when my body takes its last breath; the only difference is that I'll be taking another inhale. When focusing on the particular spatial gap between my body exhales and the next inhalation, I will come to know peace, calm, and inner joy. This is the portal for my transitioning which will erase my fear of death's illusion.

A Thought to Ponder at Dawn

When a sound or a thought enters the gap of silence during meditation, this distraction brings me back into the illusive reality of time and space.

I'm reminded of the world that I'm currently living in as well as the expanded realm which I'll eventually transition into.

I look into today with that same freedom vibration that lives inside of me.

A Thought to Ponder at Dusk

In deep silence, the awareness and connection to all that is, is clear and encompassing.

My physical body is an illusion that confirms my separation from all that is, however realizing that my physical body mimics one of an infinite number of rooms in the great house called the universe, I can embrace my connection.

Although the rooms are individually different, they are all in the Universal House.

Living in illusion can be so much fun to play in when I say that it is.

A Thought to Ponder at Dawn

All that ever was, has existed in the infinite stream of past moments, which occurred long before human creation and this stream will continue beyond anything my mind can ever comprehend.

All that was is, and will ever be, will continue long after the solar system is gone. The dramas, traumas, as well as all of the joys in life, live *only* in human existence.

Going into the universe which lives within me is a great reset from reality's illusions.

A Thought to Ponder at Dusk

People who come close to having a near-death experience have their spirits in familiar territory, yet swim in a river of forgetfulness about what it was once like to once be on the other side.

An awakened mind is aware of this and doesn't have the words to describe it purely other than to attempt to share it from their mind's vantage point.

It's not possible to accurately communicate the vastness of experiences because all languages lack the spectrum of descriptive words needed to be precise and pure. Similar to my dream state, I am familiar with sleep and yet can't put words to explain what is exactly happening with any sense of precision.

A Thought to Ponder at Dawn

Having a limited mental capacity along with an insufficient language with which to express the purity of any experience, my mind does its best to create its point of view.

Ironically, when we like what's created, we easily take the credit, yet when something occurs which is not up to par, we often look for a person or thing to point a finger at. This is quite an average behavior and not at all normal for a healthy and expanding mind.

I commit to approaching each day as the creator of my reality without exception. No matter what words I choose for things, all experiences are pure, and therefore bringing my limited interpretations to the table is at best inadequate. Therefore I will continually look to create a reality for myself that is worth living into.

A Thought to Ponder at Dusk

I experience the *truth* until the attosecond my mind steps in and removes the purity of that *experience* itself with my interpreted thoughts. Imparting my interpretation onto an experience is the reason why reality is void of *truth*. The instant interpretations are created, the *is-ness, truth*, the *experience* itself, is gone.

I've learned that living inside of illusion includes imagination and wonder, which proved to be quite incredible and very useful for Mr. Walt Disney. Perhaps it's time for me to close my eyes and visit Peter Pan.

A Thought to Ponder at Dawn

It's one thing to not find my car at a mall but needing to call security to drive me looking for it, confronts a fear that my memory is slipping.

Making myself wrong is one thing but staying stuck in that is completely another. From now on when this occurs, I find a seat, close my eyes, breathe in calmness, and go back in time and see exactly where I parked.

Remaining calm is key to making it easier to have greater memory recall. When forgetfulness combines with fear, it's dysfunctional and unkind to my psyche. I promise to practice this technique every time I find myself forgetful. The drama of being upset or judgmental no longer serves me, especially when all that's required is calming my mind and shifting my perspective.

A Thought to Ponder at Dusk

Whatever I see outside is always a complete reflection of my internal thoughts, assessments, and projections.

By not pointing the finger of blame at others or situations for all that is generated inside of my head, I will begin to own my power more steadily. The irony is that there is no going back once I've recognized this because innocence and ignorance have disappeared. Each day I create a life of my own design and thank my past for getting me to this point.

Day 196

A Thought to Ponder at Dawn

My life's lessons are whatever I say they are, nothing more and nothing less.

With eyes closed, I reflect on this past week for 5 minutes to recall what I've learned and what in fact, I'm grateful for. Reflection paired with gratitude is a priceless 'to-me, from-me' gift of consciousness.

Starting each day from this mindset alters my physiology and quality of life.

A Thought to Ponder at Dusk

A common reaction to any fearful thinking is to create a false sense of safety and security in a perceived external environment to find calm inside of my mind. Realizing that all fear-based sagas are *inside* jobs, leaves me no choice but to face them inwardly head on.

Franklin D. Roosevelt said, 'There is nothing to fear but fear itself'; the energy that vibrates behind the mind's fear influences change on a cellular level.

Some fears are paralyzing and depressing which have become as common as a cold. Like the Cowardly Lion taught us, triumph occurs by being in action in the face of fear.

A Thought to Ponder at Dawn

"I know I'm getting old when the senior citizens in television commercials look 20 years younger than I do." — anonymous

Even when they are meant to entertain, comparisons can be hurtful and harmful. Comparing identical twins, who have the same DNA, is a blow to their psyche as well.

Therefore, the precision in comparing apples to apples is nearly impossible. Meditation, yoga, and other personal private learning experiences are optimal playgrounds for self-constructive comparison while living in a world of comparisons.

A Thought to Ponder at Dusk

When I allow and accept the things which I have little or no power over, to simply be as they are, I'm in alignment with sustainable inner balance and gratitude.

Giving up resistance allows my life to flow more smoothly and easily, instead of having my fears render me powerless or stop me from being in action.

The ridiculousness of all fear-based illusions is impetus enough to alter this behavior.

A Thought to Ponder at Dawn

The energy which creates *authentic* love — the full allowance and acceptance of all that is and isn't — is readily felt when I breathe into this moment with my eyes closed.

Closing my eyes helps to remove external distractions, allowing me to focus more easily.

When peace or balance is absent, I inhale five calming breaths of those thoughts.

These breaths are the reset button that returns my heart and mind to *authentic* love.

A Thought to Ponder at Dusk

There is simplicity and awe in the process of watching fear transform.

Meeting a fear with the open arms of empathy, and compassion, along to understand its origin, fear can then stream in and out of consciousness without causing any blockages until it is nowhere to be found.

Before sleep, I choose a fear to embrace and allow to diminish without resistance; once complete, my heart and mind will realize peace once more.

A Thought to Ponder at Dawn

When I'm stuck, it's usually because I'm trying to push a door open when in fact, it works by pulling it open instead.

Today should I get stuck, I'll look for the simple solution, which is often under my nose, instead of making things more complicated.

A Thought to Ponder at Dusk

A Nighttime Mind Cleanse:

Lying awake in bed with my eyes closed, I allow *peace, calm,* and *self-acceptance,* to separately enter my body with each stream of breath (repeating 10X each).

I will breathe out any opposition to those three intentions and rotate them with each breath for a total of 30 breaths.

This practice helps prepare my mind and body for a sound and deep night's sleep.

A Thought to Ponder at Dawn

A strong and dependable new way of thinking produces a new way of living. Thoughts become things and therefore each morning, I create my day.

I can set my day before either before I step out of bed, while I'm showering, or even when brushing my teeth. Honoring my word with action is the critical deed that strengthens my integrity.

Without integrity, there is little if no workability. I will love myself by honoring my word with action and creating an unrecognizable life.

A Thought to Ponder at Dusk

Before a word is created and given an assigned definition, that which it is referring to is meaningless. Our entire reality, which includes our own story, the entire history of man and earth, the universe, and everything we know, is loaded with meaning.

We are the only species that is heavily influenced by the significance of meaning. Greater consciousness itself is void of meaning because it simply *is*.

To end my day and cleanse my mind, I close my eyes and focus solely on my breath. This puts me in alignment for a rejuvenating night's sleep.

A Thought to Ponder at Dawn

Should there be a storm today, I cannot stop it, I can't even calm it down. I can, however, calm myself and have a calmness that exists inside of every cell in my body.

A daily practice of only calmness will benefit the quality of my life in countless ways. Being non-reactive to drama or upset would be a huge accomplishment, allowing the quality of my life to be beyond imagination.

I set my daily intention to be grounded and stabilized in calm energy throughout today.

A Thought to Ponder at Dusk

Clearly stated, miracles are unknown laws of nature that exist without a scientific interpretation.

Until we can make logical sense of a miracle, there is no way to create a reality about it other than to call it a miracle.

With this understanding, I can move forward with knowing that miracles are all around me just waiting to happen and be coined into reality as new scientific facts.

A Thought to Ponder at Dawn

At some point in childhood, something significant happens which dampened my ability to live in wonder and imagination, and that sadly seems to occur for most people. How old was I when I stopped dreaming and playing like Peter Pan or thought that Disney World was just for kids? Perhaps it's time to rethink this perspective.

Although being a responsible adult requires that I hold onto my power center and remain mindful of maintaining balance in my life, it can still be exciting and a whole lot of fun. For instance, knowing who Santa Clause really is, should not stop us from teaching our kids that Santa is a *gift of generosity and giving* that lives inside of all of us. Just because I am blessed to grow old, in no way means that I have to behave that way.

A Thought to Ponder at Dusk

If speaking kindly to plants helps them to grow and thrive better, imagine what speaking kindly to people would do. With thoughts and words having a direct impact on other living things, I'm inspired to think of how I can be more compassionate and loving.

I'm ready to choose someone whom I'm not in favor of and challenge myself with what needs to happen for me to heal that relationship. Before I reach out to them tomorrow, I can clean up the dysfunction in my mind first. When I forgive myself and others for any wrongdoing, I notice a sense of freedom, lightness, and joy, not to mention a deep sense of satisfaction.

A Thought to Ponder at Dawn

Creating new words for things brings experiences to life. Creating a definition for those words gives the experience it's a heartbeat inside of reality. Definitions give words their significance and meaning, adding flavor, quality, substance, and color.

Poetry, a perfect abstract example, illustrates how our mind stops to refocus to understand the choice of words and their meanings.

Access to multiple forms of communication significantly challenges clear understanding and invites me to be more empathetic and forgiving when communications aren't clear. It's important to always be mindful and clear when communicating.

A Thought to Ponder at Dusk

The fear behind the 'what ifs' in my thinking, kills off the possibility of ever finding joy in the 'what is' and 'what's so'.

Allowing and accepting people and things to be just as they are helps me to realize that my prior focus was to wish that things were different which would play on my fears.

My focus on the 'what ifs', keeps me on the defensive, while focusing on my breath in the present moment, shifts my focus away from fear quite easily.

A Thought to Ponder at Dawn

I am the author of an amazing novel called, 'The Story of My Life.

It's an autobiography that is filled with fictitious and factual events, with each chapter representing a year in my life.

I began to have much more fun with my most recent chapters because I've realized that as I gain more wisdom, I make sure that my pen is sharing what I'd like it to say, rather than what I was taught to say. With each chapter comes a foundational platform for what is to show up next.

Although influenced by passed chapters, I'm inspired to write about anything I can dream up to create, with a similar sense of wonder and imagination to what I had in earlier chapters. My thoughts arrive from a sea of possibility knowing that a great chapter is on its way.

A Thought to Ponder at Dusk

As a person who relates to everything in the world from a subjective point of view, how is it possible for me to have an objective point of view that is void of any subjectivity?

Might I be more objective if I listened through the eyes of compassion and kindness?

I seek mindful objectivity to see how subjective my objectivity is.

A Thought to Ponder at Dawn

I am free to alter and expand my state of consciousness, yet I am not free to stop my life's expression until it's over.

No matter how many times I'd like to crawl into a hole or run away and not face my challenges, I realize that this behavior is also a part of my expression.

Life is not meant to be lived in a suppressed or restricted manner.

Those who are checked out are often paralyzed and don't always see an option to thrive.

I promise to remain aware of expressing myself and help others return to life as well.

A Thought to Ponder at Dusk

If I'm just going to do it, anything, whatever it is, I plan to do it with strong intention and heartfelt purpose, or else it's not worth wasting valuable time.

Although being unreasonable and going full out will produce uncertain results, the energetic vibration of being fully alive in the moment is priceless and rewarding.

A Thought to Ponder at Dawn

Thoughts of the unknown often heighten the fears inside of an unenlightened mind, while an enlightened mind has come to know the unknown with familiarity.

This is an opportunity to remain free and unencumbered no matter what the fear may be.

A Thought to Ponder at Dusk

Everything about me including the world around me has come into my life from words, labels, definitions, and the significance of their meaning, all of which have been made up.

This was never fine with me when I thought that I was powerless to do anything about it.

Realizing that I've always been the creator of my reality, erases the need to forgive my own ignorance and ultimately the ignorance of others, and opens the doorway to freedom and power.

A Thought to Ponder at Dawn

Believing in the illusion of an *absolute truth* perpetuates fear, victimization, disharmony, and hatred, not to mention prevents having authentic love and peace in my life.

Out of all my hidden *truths*, which big one do I still hold as *true*?

Hint for the answer: 'What do I complain about the most or am not ever happy with?'

Once I realize this, the space is created for transformation to occur.

A Thought to Ponder at Dusk

My ability to always choose good over things that are not, requires conscious effort.

As the creator of my own life's mirage, I'm able to recognize my ignorance when I allow thoughts that are unkind, unhealthy, and unsatisfying.

Once awareness kicks in, I can opt to create whatever brings good health, abundance, prosperity, freedom, and joy into my life.

A Thought to Ponder at Dawn

I will set my intention on something that I'd like to see happen and then I'll generate a thought in my head to recall throughout the day to remain conscious of it.

I have the option of enrolling others in my vision or privately living inside of my intention.

This will require me to think more, speak less, and be in action.

A Thought to Ponder at Dusk

My feelings are a direct response and reflective of the thoughts in my mind. When my mind thinks, it causes my physical body to react on a cellular level.

This reaction can create a physical feeling that I may not be aware of.

I can then choose to close my eyes, relax my body, and conduct a full body scan, looking for blockages or areas of internal discomfort; body scanning is a cool and fun thing to do!

When found, I can embrace those areas with my mind and watch them slip away. When completed, my night's slumber is often deep and restful.

A Thought to Ponder at Dawn

When I close my eyes, I can feel and sometimes hear my heartbeat. The awareness of my heartbeat is remarkable because it beats for my sustenance. This small and precious organ tirelessly spreads life energy to my entire body. Although it beats to its own rhythm, sometimes it joins with others in unison.

I love and care for my heartbeat and by deepening my awareness of my heart's energy, I understand the magnitude of its purpose. Thoughts of love may be generated in my mind, but my heart is the center of love and representation of a lifetime flow of giving and receiving of life to my body.

A Thought to Ponder at Dusk

I relate to people based on meaningful perspectives that I hold about them. This fixed perspective cuts off the possibility of them ever being someone else otherwise.

The moment that I give up my solidly held vantage point, I open a space to explore seeing and relating to them in a new and more generous manner.

On the flip side, others will hold solid impressions of me that I can do nothing about, so I'll focus on altering my made-up opinions of others by creating new ones and interacting with them differently.

A Thought to Ponder at Dawn

All reality is created by adding meaningful interpretations to pure experiences. Significant and traumatic challenges that occur in childhood are often the motivator to become an advocate for those with similar interpretations.

Although experiences are happenstance, the agreement to hold similar perspectives is what keeps the stories credible, meaningful, signif- icant, and alive.

Creating a new perspective that frees up any energetic trauma takes the admission that what was initially interpreted wasn't true, although real, thereby making it possible to recreate a new perspective.

A Thought to Ponder at Dusk

Being stuck or upset about something occurs because of a hidden *truth* I'm harboring. For instance, reflecting on relationships that had ended poorly, I can ask myself an amazing question: 'What *truth* might I still be harboring about that person or the relationship, that if I gave it up right now, I'd be completely freed up from it?"

By choosing from an infinite sea of realities, I can put a new perspective in place that will leave me more empowered, allowing me to forgive those involved, and return to peace.

A Thought to Ponder at Dawn

During the process of enlightenment, a mind comes to understand the absence of *truth* in human reality — all meanings that are created or agreed upon are universal illusions. For instance, a tree is only a tree because we agree that it's a tree, yet a tree will never know that it's a tree.

Yoga and meditation provide a reprieve from constant thinking, allowing mindlessness to recognize peace and joy; although void of *truth*, it is an *authentic* creation (when *authenticity* replaces the concept of having any *truth*, in reality, freedom appears).

Creating a new reality that is more valuable, more nourishing, and even more rewarding than the one I currently live in, occurs when I choose to create a new illusion.

A Thought to Ponder at Dusk

Mind-clearing is not a practice that is commonly found anywhere at home or in school, nor is it a favorite activity that most people do on a Saturday night. Why Not? Mind-clearing is associated with meditation and occurs as not fun or difficult to do. It is critical for maintaining a healthy mind and is worth doing every day.

Consider creating a meditation group and include singing bowls, music, chanting, and even drumming as ways to make a mind-clearing practice pleasant and worthwhile. No matter what, I am committed to a life-long practice of clearing my mind because it's nourishing and rejuvenating.

A Thought to Ponder at Dawn

Embracing *nothingness* is like having a master key to expanding consciousness. Reality comes with a collective way of living where the abundance of people, places, and things makes it improbable to enjoy daily peace and calm in a practice of nothingness.

This is a reason why seekers join monasteries, and convents, go on spiritual retreats and seek other ways, including meditation and prayer, to cleanse and calm the mind. Overstimulation can short-circuit the healthiest of minds at times. Every living thing exerts energy and finds ways to rest and regenerate to survive. An ideal cleanse is to return to mindlessness — nothingness — as a daily practice, where I am renewed, and anything is possible once more.

A Thought to Ponder at Dusk

Words without definition are viewed as powerless; my agreement and participation in the meaning given to a word, however, is where the big punch of energetic intention exists. Before words and meanings are created, the energy behind thoughts and feelings do still exist, although the longevity and magnitude of their impact would most likely diminish.

There would not be a story to tell or anything to hold onto. Understanding this thought process is a beautiful and powerful way to end my day because I can let go of if only temporarily, the words and meanings that bind me. With a breath, I calm my mind and body and honor the nightly reset that it deserves.

A Thought to Ponder at Dawn

Recognizing that my veil of ignorance cuts off awareness that anyone's reality is righter or better than mine allows me to seek out advice from others more easily.

Others may have a clearer view than mine, especially when they can see from a more neutral perspective, which can allow me to incorporate theirs as my own. Being open-minded has never hurt me and has given me great strides in my development.

As a child, I was blessed to live inside of wonder and imagination and like a sponge, take in information. Today I will challenge myself to place serious focus on learning something from anything by looking through my child's eyes.

A Thought to Ponder at Dusk

Fearing death won't stop my exit, but it can interfere with and prevent me from living. In addition, worrying hasn't taken away or altered my tomorrow's troubles, but they sure have taken away today's moments of calm and peace.

Refocusing thoughts is an answer to recreating a new perspective within which to live. Clearing my mind is often easier to address when I'm ready for the dream state.

My mind releases the day's thoughts when I breathe in peace and say goodbye to them.

A Thought to Ponder at Dawn

A breakdown of any size or magnitude breaks through when I face what's upsetting me. By willfully removing the *truth* from my story about it, I can release any strongly held interpretation which has rendered me powerless.

Breakthroughs, however still untrue, usually occur on their own and usually immediately following a breakdown and allow me to create a new illusory perspective to live into. What challenges can I recall to meet head-on, to cherish a breakthrough?

A Thought to Ponder at Dusk

To achieve advancement, I embrace the intelligence in others, notice what's lacking in mine, and acknowledge them for being a part of my learning process.

I close my eyes and recall those who've taught me valuable life lessons and bow to them in gratitude, realizing that some of them haven't a clue of how awesome they are.

My level of gratitude runs fairly deep and brings me lasting joy.

A Thought to Ponder at Dawn

Giving advice is something that comes easily and effortlessly.

The question is, "What advice can I give to myself, such that it will position me to live a healthier and happier day today and every day, and with a whole lot more fun?"

It might be as simple as committing to honor myself more by having my actions match my words of good intention.

A Thought to Ponder at Dusk

In chatting with someone, I may say to them, 'You're nothing without- out people's assessments and interpretations of you — this includes your own as well. The same holds for myself, 'I am nothing without other folk's assessment of me.'

Realizing that we simply *are* what *we are* and that I *am* that *I am*, removes the labels, the beliefs, and the identity, leaving me with what? Nada! What would life be like if life's illusions didn't exist? Not only would it be mind-boggling, but it'd also be most freeing.

How significantly do I relate to things and how reactionary am I as a result? How do I wrap my brain around the realization that all interpretations are fictitious?

A Thought to Ponder at Dawn

Giving up the *truth* about what I make things mean, places me in the realm of infinite possibility from which to choose another point of view that works more optimally.

Understanding that this is access to power and freedom is incredible.

Living my life from this perspective is emancipating, gratifying, and a slice of heaven.

A Thought to Ponder at Dusk

I know I'm getting old when I haven't seen one Academy Award-nominated movie. Growing old doesn't have to mean anything negative, especially when it's inevitable.

I, therefore, welcome my aging process and seek to remain in the world of the living. Mingling with younger generations is ideal for this kind of inspiration and engagement.

Senior communities have their advantages, although they hinder the flow of integration. How old I behave directly influences how old I feel and therefore why it's important to behave with wonder, inquiry, and imagination.

A Thought to Ponder at Dawn

Allowing myself to be fearful over anything that inevitably occurs, like death, gives it unnecessary power over me and is a gross waste of precious time and energy.

Although fears haven't killed me, the fear of fears has indoctrinated me into the world of the living dead, brought on dis-ease, and hastened my aging process.

I will embrace my fears, remain in forward action regardless, and not allow fear to steal away any more of my life's most precious moments.

I will also trigger myself to add fun and comedy alongside every fear.

A Thought to Ponder at Dusk

Gratitude and thankfulness are two words with powerful associated meanings that can alter the energy vibration of a cell and result in a physiological shift.

What five things can I bring to mind that I am grateful for?

With my eyes closed, I will breathe into each of them with a slow and focused breath and be present with how they feel and settle into my body while I enter my sleep world.

A Thought to Ponder at Dawn

The world of *self-help* is a multi-million-dollar industry and fills a universal void for people who believe that they're not 'good enough' in some manner.

Countless quick and easy fixes are written, published, and sold.

Their lifespan usually lasts between six to twelve months before something new appears.

Realizing that I was never broken and always good enough, I'm able to live more freely. Fad diets, pill-popping solutions, cosmetic procedures, and anything which reinforces the idea of my lack, take their proper place in the garbage heap. I am a work in progress and any unkind self-assessment indicates a call for my return to my power center which properly realigns my commitment to health and wellness.

A Thought to Ponder at Dusk

Like a diamond, all of the facets which make up my identity have an opportunity to shine. The facets which are clear and clean shine brilliantly while others just remain unclear.

I address my dark spots with focused attention for them to shine brighter. My brilliance is my responsibility and is the best thing that I give to myself and others.

A Thought to Ponder at Dawn

Whenever my interpretations of an experience become the *way it is*, the illusion of *truth* embeds itself into my belief system and all that is infinitely possible is lost.

As the gamekeeper of my life, I will give greater leniency to larger challenges. I will not allow any beliefs to be so structured that it prevents my life from flowing easily.

Being aware of the transitory flow of life, I am mindful of what I still hold as permanent. This helps me to stay committed to living in my own creation of reality and not the *truth*.

A Thought to Ponder at Dusk

I'm always a choice away from enjoying a life of my own design because I solely remain in charge of my life's story; I get to keep what I like and rewrite what I don't.

My life is the biggest game to play, and I play it my way.

I refuse to feel burdened with *fixing* anything because nothing was ever broken, perhaps only poorly written, and therefore may simply require a rewrite.

A Thought to Ponder at Dawn

A person's behavior towards me is solely a reflection of how they view their world; knowing that the same holds for me, underscores the importance of being responsible.

My daily challenge, however, is to consistently react in kindness, compassion, and love, no matter if the behavior is positive or negative. Maintaining my center of power is vital in holding my position of non-reactivity and mastering this behavior allows me the opportunity to live in heaven on earth.

A Thought to Ponder at Dusk

An amazing characteristic of *reality* is that it's always changing behind the scenes, whether or not you want it to, and is reinforced by having the concepts of time and space embedded into it. The concept of ultimate *truth*, however, which is the *is-ness* of all things, exists outside of reality and remains as a constant *is-ness* because time and space are absent.

The *is-ness*, which is whatever *it is*, can shift and whenever it does, still remains whatever *it is* and continues on without an associated reality attached to it. Saying *I Am* that *I Am* and *it is* what *it is*, leaves no way of relating to its essence of *truth*.

The moment I give meaning to something that *is*, the *truth* is instantly substituted with reality, making it real, meaningful, and significant, and how we all relate to things.

Day 221

A Thought to Ponder at Dawn

Survival is not a function of strength or intellect; it is based on flexibility and adaptability. Adaptation is both congenital as well as behavior that is learned in childhood.

When I run and seek refuge from fear, I learn little about being resourceful. Facing fear allows me to adjust, giving me to navigate through life more easily.

Using fear as a tool to expand consciousness helps me to be more flexible and adaptive.

A Thought to Ponder at Dusk

The world and everyone in it owe me nothing.

Without expectation, abundance and prosperity flow effortlessly.

There's contentment and joy when I remember things that I'm grateful for.

I can also choose to focus on all that's missing and remain unhappy.

A Thought to Ponder at Dawn

It's hard for me to forget someone special nor would I want to, especially if their life has positively touched mine.

I take this moment to recall five people, whether dead or alive, whose presence has brought unexpected fun, joy, and laughter, into my life.

While I'm smiling, I'm thinking of who I can be for today.

A Thought to Ponder at Dusk

When I want something, I successfully get to have the *wanting* or craving of it, rather than having the thing itself. For example, all that insomniacs ever want is to fall asleep, and ruminating about it, yields wanting to fall asleep because that's their focus.

Shifting their focus to other things will eventually allow them to fall asleep. Oftentimes when I intensely focus on something, it usually occurs, why?

Knowing that what I focus my mind on, usually grows and expands, what shall I place my focus on?

A Thought to Ponder at Dawn

We all have our own opinions about people, places, and things.

What I choose to share about them, however, tells my listener what they can expect I'll be sharing about them in their absence.

Without fixing this character glitch, what must I be aware of not to gossip anymore?

Compassion? Empathy? Kindness? Genuine Caring? Respectful Friendship? Love?

I responsibly move forward by forgiving myself for not realizing this perspective sooner.

A Thought to Ponder at Dusk

When I find myself stuck with anything, I'm imprisoned by the illusion of holding a subconscious *truth* about something or someone.

Seeing it as being real or significant, I can quickly choose a new point of view.

An empowering vantage point allows my center strength to return, usually resulting in a greater sense of freedom and happiness.

A Thought to Ponder at Dawn

The impact of knowing that my autobiography is an amazing novel filled with an array of fictional chapters allows me the freedom to create and enjoy any reality that I so choose.

The idea that the absolute *truth* exists in anyone's reality is not only the greatest blunder our species has ever made, but it's also an impossibility.

Whenever I find myself stuck, I find comfort in remembering Carl Sagan's quote, "Reality is an illusion, albeit a persistent one."

And boy is it ever!

A Thought to Ponder at Dusk

"The meaning of life is to find your gift. The purpose of life is to give it away." —Pablo Picasso

Life simply is what *it is*, and I then make it mean whatever I want or agree to; my purpose is also whatever I make up and say that it is.

Embracing my life in this manner and every moment of every day, powerfully choosing how I see things, I'd be unrecognizable even to myself hands down. Although I may not succeed at first, I just might want to have fun giving it a go.

A Thought to Ponder at Dawn

Placing blame on anyone or anything is irresponsible for the reality that I've created. Blame occurs in multiple forms; in silence or withholding, in withdrawal and anger, in complacency and shame, and it never leads to anything worthwhile.

Claiming my power as the creator of my reality makes anything possible. Holding myself accountable is more burdensome, a lot more work, and my only choice is if I want to thrive and not be part of the living dead. Any unpleasant karma is my reminder for better choices to make and actions to take.

A Thought to Ponder at Dusk

Being fully alive begins at the edge of my comfort zone. I don't need to go bungee jumping or sky diving to break through my fears, however, it would be helpful to look at where I'm still playing it safe in my life.

When I play cautiously, I receive just that… safety, soundness, and little excitement. When I choose to take educated risks to free myself from complacency, paralysis, and the quicksand of indecision, a rippling effect of exuberance is felt.

I have only one life, one identity, and one body; how much freedom and joy will I create? My evenings are times of reflection, while my days are moments for action.

A Thought to Ponder at Dawn

My reality was created and shaped from inherited and adopted beliefs, which have grown strong as a result of perpetuation and validation, yet not one bit of *truth*. Coming from a certain cultural background, my story about things is therefore skewed.

This challenges me to see things with clear objectivity and causes me to slip focus by assuming that other people see things the way I see them. Never mind the impossibility of anyone seeing anything in the same manner, any action to persuade others into seeing things my way, it's usually met with great resistance.

For me to find a common ground, it's best that I seek to understand others first. Whenever I feel listened to and understood, it's easier for me to listen more clearly. I choose this method of communicating as a great way of connecting with people.

A Thought to Ponder at Dusk

As a child, our mind is clear, empty, inquisitive, and filled with wonder, and all that is possible lives inside of our young and innocent minds. Any perspective held as *true* is bound, imprisoned, and loses access to possibility.

I welcome conflicts that lead to a *breakdown*, to process any unpleasant thoughts as a catalyst, and the perfect opportunity to witness a *breakthrough* in perspective. Creating new thought streams circumvents discomfort generated from beliefs in *truth*, dysfunctional thinking, and falling short of what I'm passionate about.

A Thought to Ponder at Dawn

No matter what, no two energetic pathways are ever identical. This is even the case for identical twins where their DNA is exactly the same. Every mind and body allow for its expression of the same experience.

Every member of any group, organization, or community has their own version of what it is like to be in that culture; although similar, there are no two identical realities. This uniqueness pulls my focus, causing me to forget that we are all the same. In addition to the oneness of spirit, everything comes from the same cosmic stardust. I only remain an individual expression of thought and creation until it's time to transition. When I return to the infinite and eternal connection to *all that is*, I am home.

A Thought to Ponder at Dusk

Reality is right, meaningful, significant, valuable, and yet always remains *truthless*. Everything about me was made up from the time I was born — my name, my social security number, my daily schedules and timelines, my entire inherited ancestry, and all the customary 'ways' of living my life, none of which I had any say over. Yet without my identity, I wouldn't know who I am.

Not realizing there was ever a choice, I adopted all of it as true, hook line, and sinker. Before sleep, I will intentionally step out of my identity's **B**elief **S**ystem (reality) like a wet suit to feel pounds lighter and create a new portal to my dream state. As I recreate myself, what three things will I like to see happen for myself? My dream state awaits, and I may consider journaling about it first thing tomorrow.

A Thought to Ponder at Dawn

No matter what the situation, my reality is given by how my mind interprets things. This explains why no two realities can ever be the same when the experience itself is.

What stops me from choosing a better perspective when I know how this dynamic works? It is the repetitive practice of interpretation over time that falsely generates a *truth*.

This is a huge mistake that often costs me freedom and happiness.

A Thought to Ponder at Dusk

Awareness: A child has little awareness of what's going on around them and far greater awareness of what's happening right in front of them.

As we mature, peripheral awareness and consciousness develop nicely, yet a shift back to childhood seems to occur for many, not all, seniors entering their twilight years.

Although speculation is made as to why this occurs for some and not others, the final turnout remains a mystery.

A Thought to Ponder at Dawn

My identity is a result of a custom-built and highly personalized mind which was imprinted upon me by adults long before I had any say about how things were going to go. Understanding this inspires me to recreate aspects of myself that don't work for me, but being left without clear instruction, makes it all the more challenging.

Most forms of learning occur as a result of repetition and mastery which is achieved as a result of one's demeanor and personal approach to learning. The quote, 'fake it till you make it', is OK, but not really empowering.

Learning anything new takes time, patience, and determination, so instead of 'faking it til I make it', I'd rather, "Believe it, till I See it." As a 'Success, waiting to happen, with practice and will, I can "Be the change that I wish to see", (a famous quote by Gandhi).

A Thought to Ponder at Dusk

All scientific discovery calls upon my imagination to offer an understanding of what was once unknown — meanings and circumstances usually precede the invented names. For example, at birth, I was whatever I was, but it didn't end there.

Everything in human reality, including meanings, names, rules, etc, would soon blanket and shape my world without my knowledge or approval. My mind can't erase all of the years as chapters in my life's autobiography, nor would I want to, but with the power of my imagination, I can create new ones from now on.

A Thought to Ponder at Dawn

Reality is infinite and always in flux because nothing stays the same.

Truth never changes because the very nature of its definition is that *it is what it is*. Anything perceived as *truth* that then changes was never true, to begin with. Although *truth* and reality are valid and significant, one holds a life sentence.

This is a tough concept to comprehend because of how we are trained. 'Swearing, to tell the truth, the whole truth, and nothing but the truth, so help me God?', is simply impossible although 'Swearing to tell my authentic reality, my entire perspective, and nothing but my point of view, so help me God', is possible. When I fully understand this, I become fully responsible for owning my vantage point.

A Thought to Ponder at Dusk

Character is having the ability to follow through on a decision, after the fanfare of the moment is long gone and no one is watching. Character building is a huge benefit to me because it helps strengthen my power center.

When I'm not aware of my center core, my integrity often goes fishing. This game of life is simple to play only when I honor my words with appropriate actions. This lesson is fully learned when there's no one around.

A Thought to Ponder at Dawn

Whenever I want something badly enough, I usually find a way to get it. Conversely, when I say that I want something but don't want it, no matter how convincing I may be, it doesn't seem to happen.

Willful action generates results while trying usually never meets the mark and yet, either way, I'm still creating a reality. The statement, "I'm trying" is a universal communication that expresses good intentions but is often accompanied by inauthentic undertones.

Catching the words "I'm trying" will be a trigger for me to examine my intention. I'll also pay closer attention to when others respond to me in this manner.

A Thought to Ponder at Dusk

The process of transformation hosts an alternate consciousness that generates new thoughts into a new reality and therefore, whenever it's time to close the book on a particular point of view, it is accomplished by altering the current perspective.

A new vantage point comes as a result of recognizing the illusion of the reality at hand. Access to power and freedom appears the moment I recognize that my entire life's reality has been an illusion from birth and hold onto this awareness for the rest of my days.

This will make it easier to uncover illusions that I still hold as *true*.

A Thought to Ponder at Dawn

Logical and scientific thinking doesn't usually pay attention to the fear of the inevitable.

This mindset lives in the exploration of wonder and the excitement of discovery.

Fearing the unknown often skews, sometimes paralyzes, a mind's thought process and remains a most amazing conundrum because possibility lives inside of the unknown.

Authentic creations come from nothing and will be my challenge today.

A Thought to Ponder at Dusk

Not being known or understood doesn't stop a miracle from being a miracle.

A miracle is nothing more than an unknown law or uncharted logic. Miracles exist everywhere, including in my dream state.

When I'm ready for bed, I will focus on putting peace, calm, and miracles into my body one at a time until I am satiated by them.

I will be mindful not to focus on anything else until I'm fast asleep.

A Thought to Ponder at Dawn

The creation of the illusory words, *I*, *me*, and *my*, are reasons why there is even a conversation about *oneness* in the first place. Without adding the *self* to a conversation, the need to distinguish *oneness* disappears.

Individuality permeates inside all human reality as a way to distinguish, separate, and honor our uniqueness under the umbrella of one humanity.

The importance of realizing that all reality is made up can help us not to take life too seriously and put a little playtime and fun into the mix.

A Thought to Ponder at Dusk

All of the thoughts which continue to give rise to everything in my current *belief system* are not the same thought process that will allow transformation or my consciousness to expand.

It is a thoughtless mind which can access an amazing expansion of consciousness.

Mindlessness is an enormous gift that my mind can give to itself; it takes time, costs nothing, and is one of the most priceless gifts that I can ever give to myself.

A Thought to Ponder at Dawn

Transformation allows access to a greater awareness that allows alternative perspectives to generate new thoughts into new realities.

With all that is possible, what new things can I passionately create today?

A Thought to Ponder at Dusk

In my reality, who I am is a reflection of both, whom you and I say that I am.

Suffice it to say, I am validated by collective opinion when I buy into that underlying agreement.

What have I subconsciously agreed to that no longer serves me and am willing to give up?

A Thought to Ponder at Dawn

Blessed are those who see the beauty in things that they powerfully believe in and hold no *truth* about.

Beauty is collectively agreed upon, it is both objective and subjective and literally in the eyes and minds of those who behold it.

What I find beautiful, others may be in complete opposition about, and we are both right.

A Thought to Ponder at Dusk

My reality, as well as my identity, have been inherited, adopted, and perpetuated.

They all constitute my entire "B"elief "S"ystem, which conveniently exposes the obvious acronym, *B.S.*.

My entire belief system - *B.S.* - is all that I have.

Contrary to popular belief, there is not or has ever been a *Truth System* or *T.S.* The huge benefit of this knowledge is that it allows me to take any of my antiquated or unhealthy past interpretations and recreate something new which empowers me and brings me joy. In short, this is a great portal to my emancipation.

A Thought to Ponder at Dawn

When awake, I create interpretations that are of optimal service to myself and humanity.

This surrounds me with a gratifying sense of power and accomplishment.

What challenge is still lurking in my space that needs cleaning up and enlightening which will clear the way for me to conjure up something awesome for today's contribution?

A Thought to Ponder at Dusk

Self-Realization is present when engagement and detachment are simultaneously in play and indifference is the perspective that neutralizes all positive or negative charges from my interpretations.

Assimilating the wisdom of non-reactivity allows peace and freedom to alter my physiology on a cellular level.

Day 237

A Thought to Ponder at Dawn

In public and group settings, my mind searches to figure out where it best fits in.

Structurally blinded to our *oneness*, many people feel separated from others and do everything they can to belong which is one of the many ironies of reality's illusion.

What will it take for me to make a permanent shift into the oneness that I'm already living in, to easily access fun and freedom inside of the world of illusion that I already live in?

A Thought to Ponder at Dusk

Being in the *now* disappears time and space and meditation helps me realize this. During the stillness and quiet of meditation, I shift from *Kronos* (chronological) time, where the clock keeps ticking, to *Kairos* (now or perfect) time, where time stands still.

Remembering back on when I've been so engrossed in someone or something, that time seemed to have either stood still or I got lost in time and space, that was kairos time.

Although we normally live in Kronos time during the day, the beauty of kairos time can be felt right before and during sleep by focusing on my breath.

Day 238

A Thought to Ponder at Dawn

When the fear of uncertainty shifts into authentic love (acceptance and allowance) and trusting that the unknown is possible, my mind can see that *I am* the *light* of awareness.

Daily living is not the arena for strengthening this perspective and why it's essential to take moments of quiet and alone time to be mindful of this.

Time spent realizing that the unknown can be exciting can add balance to my day.

A Thought to Ponder at Dusk

Being on a long continuous journey to enlightenment is as much of an illusion as being at the starting point of every moment.

The difference is that one illusion just keeps the freshness alive.

I am always exactly where I am, wherever it is that I am.

Where am I and how aware will I allow myself to be right now and for how long?

A Thought to Ponder at Dawn

Knowing about being in the moment and being in the moment are two separate things.

When focused on the moment, my mind is unaware that it's even in the moment.

Although knowing and being are valuable and essential, being is what generates the quality of my human life.

How I am being and behaving determines what actions I then take and the difference I make.

It's all about balance.

A Thought to Ponder at Dusk

Things that have mattered in the past and continue to directly impact my current state of affairs are good indications of my most probable and certain future.

Inside of this illusion, I have the option to choose otherwise and then be in action to alter and create a new trajectory.

A Thought to Ponder at Dawn

What's the definition of Enlightenment?

Enlightenment is the existence of an awakened mind-state of conscious clarity, realizing that being in every moment is not only like living in a heaven on earth, but it is also recognizing being in the dream state itself. Living inside of a life-long illusion allows me to create anything that I choose.

The greatest part of this is that I don't have to wait until I'm fully enlightened to begin, although if what I do create doesn't last, I'll know why. With devotion and practice, I can be unstoppable with my own creations.

A Thought to Ponder at Dusk

Every average mind comes with an identity and an accompanying ego. Its contents were inherited and then perpetuated based on repetitious thinking. An *awakened* mind, on the other hand, is emancipated from the fictitious entanglement that was once governed by its own rules and regulations.

Striking the mind's content is impossible nor is it necessary for awakening to occur. Embracing my life's autobiography as a wonderful novel instead of non-fiction will allow me to create new chapters based on possibility and pure inspiration.

Day 241

A Thought to Ponder at Dawn

The community, the culture, and even the environment in which I live provide the level of nourishment needed for my personal growth and happiness.

I'm a product of my environment and directly influenced by it. Having the ability to self-reflect and assess whether or not my environment is healthy, I can alter things within my environment to move from it completely.

It's important to be mindful of the environmental beliefs living inside of my head as well. Hosting any toxic beliefs can be paralyzing if they are dysfunctional enough. Meditation is an optimal resource that can allow me the mental reset needed. What in my environment needs my immediate love and attention?

A Thought to Ponder at Dusk

The average mind believes that the world it sees outside creates its reality, when in fact the mind's reality *is* what produces the world that it sees outside.

A Thought to Ponder at Dawn

The world outside *is* the mirrored reflection of my mind's belief system.

Everything that I think, feel, and say about what is on the outside and on the inside for that matter, is always generated inside of my mind. Whatever my interpretations are, the exact story and image of what my mind projects at every moment.

Although I may not always be responsible for it, I am the 'gatekeeper' of my thoughts; thoughts that are unworthy of projection can be left to go unspoken, while thoughts which will further growth and development, can be shared.

A Thought to Ponder at Dusk

Enlightened beings live in an awakened state of infinite connection and neutrality.

The challenge in getting to that point is easier when I am mindful that everything which is created by my mind's reality is always an illusion.

Being upset about anything is my test and returning to my awareness of life's illusion is my resolve.

A Thought to Ponder at Dawn

The expansion of consciousness begins at the end of my comfort zone. Placing importance on feelings and emotions overrides exploration into uncharted territory which can be exciting.

Similar to sports, the degree of potential danger along with the unknown is directly proportional to the level of endorphins that rush through and thrill the body.

Leaving my comfort zone, places all of my senses on high alert, causing me to be more present to everything around me. Wild animals often live on high alert and thrive outside of their comfort zone.

A Thought to Ponder at Dusk

Getting from *here to there* is an illusion of time and space which is perpetuated by thoughts of an imaginary future that is expressed in the present moment.

When tomorrow comes occurs, it is actually now, proving that tomorrow never comes. We also bring the illusory thought of yesterday's planning into our present moment.

Giving power and credit to a past and a future defines the quality of life and allows it to either positively advance on many levels or cause potential harm. Living inside of reality's illusion, I can customize it instantly at any moment by where I place my focus and attention.

A Thought to Ponder at Dawn

In an enlightening moment, I am the shift of consciousness itself.

Strengthening this energetic muscle causes a shift on a cellular and physiological level.

I can't predict its arrival; I can only embrace the illuminating process when it comes.

In preparation for enlightening moments, I commit myself to stay awake.

A Thought to Ponder at Dusk

When my mind is upset, it is still living inside of thoughts that have passed.

When my mind is anxious, it's dancing with future thoughts yet to be realized.

When I ask my mind to focus on my body's breath, inhaling and exhaling for just 5-10 minutes, my body returns to peace.

Longer moments of breath concentration allow my mind to clear itself of thought, allowing my physiology to recognize calm and contentment.

A Thought to Ponder at Dawn

Should any man look down upon another, let it be to only extend a helping hand.

As I create my day, I will be conscious of those who may need a hand.

I am mindful of my selfishness as these acts nourish my soul and bring me joy. I'm also clear that the only expectation I will set is my sense of accomplishment.

Expressions of their gratitude will be unnecessary although welcomed.

A Thought to Ponder at Dusk

It is important to remain flexible in mind and body as a sign of health and well-being.

Part of that flexibility is being open for continual shifts to occur.

Meditation is the practice that exercises the mind by helping it to find a mindless state. The absence of thought allows new perspectives to be present.

When given the same respect and consideration as the old reality, the new realm of thinking ushers in a deep sense of freedom and unbridled joy.

A Thought to Ponder at Dawn

Creating new words can language support expanding consciousness. This process may vary and sometimes requires creating new words along with new meanings, while other times it may only require giving new meaning to existing words.

New words gain foundational strength through enrollment and collective agreement. Every word in language has been made up and given meaning, giving people, places, and things, some level of significance, credibility, and strength. By understanding this process, the strength and significance may also be reduced or altered should words and meanings be toxic, obsolete, or no longer useful.

A Thought to Ponder at Dusk

My Reality and point of view are usually right pretty much. Even when I'm wrong, I'm right about that too. If my reality is designed and conducted in that manner, so must everyone else's.

The idea then of trying to persuade others that my reality is brighter than theirs is daunting. Having a collective agreement is similar but still not the same because everyone has their individual perspective about things. For example, 10 million judges, doctors, Christians, mechanics, and artists, all have their own opinion on how they live their life inside of those beliefs, and not one is identical.

A Thought to Ponder at Dawn

I have never felt myself to be authentically beautiful or worthy of adoration.

Then one day I realized that the magnificent beauty of my spirit lives in others because everything I see is, in fact, a reflection of me — the good, bad, and the ugly.

This awareness is humbling because I get to see that I'm everything, nothing, and neither.

Who today can I help see their beauty?

A Thought to Ponder at Dusk

Non-judgmental *cause-and-effect* relationships are seen in the natural order of things.

Dynamics that are intrinsic to creation itself include unknown cosmic law aka, miracles.

When considering what life would be like if my mind wasn't wired to think stuff up, I'd be completely stopped in my tracks without anything to compare or know how to relate

As I focus on my breath and remove all thoughts from my mind, I return to the *cause* of my breath and the *effect* it has on my body.

A Thought to Ponder at Dawn

One of the greatest self-induced tragedies for me to ever confront is not when I aim too high and miss, but when I aim a little too low and hit.

Setting my own limits is what I'm both responsible and guilty of.

The irony is that mindfulness equals limitlessness and yet when I monitor the resistance of my thoughts, my reflex has shifted toward continually expanding my reach.

A Thought to Ponder at Dusk

No University on earth offers a degree program for Infinite Wisdom. Wisdom is sourced from within, while scholastic knowledge is interpreted from without.

This shines a different light on the quote, "If you don't go within, you go without". Knowledge is to the mind, as wisdom is to the soul.

When I learn from scholars who came before me, I'm a devoted student of knowledge.

When I am quiet and still and go deep within, I am the teacher as well as the student.

A Thought to Ponder at Dawn

Speaking *generatively* is an inspiration for what is new and not a fix for what is old.

My challenge for today is to speak as generatively as I possibly can which can mean saying things in a new way or creating sentences that have never been spoken before.

This will take conscious thinking because generative speaking is very different and will take me being creative, innovative, and playing inside of an expanded mindset.

A Thought to Ponder at Dusk

As a collective consciousness, we all agree to believe that who we are, is generated from thoughts about who both we and others believe we are.

Repetition is a proven source of mastering greatness and amazing things and is also to blame for our demise when that which we collectively believe about ourselves is toxic. As a result, I bid farewell to any belief which doesn't further my health and well-being.

As I enter my dream state, with each breath in, I repeatedly create possibility, and with each breath out, I say rapid-fire good riddance to that which is toxic.

A Thought to Ponder at Dawn

The illusion of time and space significantly colors our lives. All starting points create an illusion suggesting that there is somewhere to get to. Something called, *over there*, makes it possible to go from point A to point B.

Spiritual teachers, however, teach the *here and now*, with no place to get to. It's normal for multiple interpretations from the same experience to exist simultaneously.

Whether it involves large groups of people or just two individuals, each person has their own reality that produces their own vantage point which is correct for them.

A Thought to Ponder at Dusk

Despite any attempts to control my thoughts, following them is a challenge. Being the observer of my thought stream opens the doorway to self-awareness.

It's a blessing when I'm able to embrace the realization that I am not my mind but in fact, the spectator of thoughts that creates my reality.

Those moments when I'm able to catch and flow with my mind's thought stream are not only incredible but have caused me to belly laugh at the silliness of it all.

A Thought to Ponder at Dawn

Being awake opens a perspective that is outside the realm of usual thinking. Recognizing myself as a *spirit* allows me to sit front row center in a virtual theatre and watch my mind and body put on an amazing live performance.

I recognize the direct influence that my mind's thoughts have on my body's response. When I'm happy, my body is happy, when my mind is challenged, unclear, and upset, my body is in dis-ease.

These cause-and-effect relationships last for a lifetime and are worth being mindful of.

A Thought to Ponder at Dusk

Permitting myself to powerfully surrender to *go deeper into the flow* of my mind's thoughts, allows the richness of life to soar beyond imagination as I willfully embrace the possibility of uncertainty and the unknown.

Surrendering helps me to understand the dynamic process of shifting my mind from the cockpit into a passenger seat for spectator purposes only.

I'm privileged to watch the gamut from my mind's brilliance to its insane stupidity. This opportunity far surpasses sitting in VIP seats at any Broadway show!

A Thought to Ponder at Dawn

Life and Death are the same in that they are both illusions. My complete identity and reality are made up as well.

Knowing is one thing however when I finally allow myself to embody this realization, I will enjoy a lifetime of freedom and happiness.

A Thought to Ponder at Dusk

The art of failing is a powerful tool when distinguished as not having any bearing or influence on one's identity and self-worth.

Failure allows me to comprehend what's missing for corrections and advancements to be made.

When I welcome failure, I welcome growth and development.

A Thought to Ponder at Dawn

Fear, a created mind perspective, causes spontaneous reactions out of an illusory need for safety and security.

The irony? Both the stimulus (fear), and the response (reactive behavior), are often fictitious.

A Thought to Ponder at Dusk

Being a committed source for everyone to live an extraordinary life is not a core sentiment of an enlightened individual, that's more sentiment for a motivational speaker.

An enlightened mind, on the other hand, focuses on creating their path, and should the life they lead, inspire others, it is an added benefit.

After hearing over and over that, "God helps those who help themselves.", it becomes clear that no one is coming to save or assist me with any of my internal challenges.

It's not even up to me to find my way, but rather to create my path by turning my focus inward to see what I'm passionate about.

What am I passionate about that deserves my time and brings joy and fulfillment?

Day 254

A Thought to Ponder at Dawn

How many multiple times, in hindsight, of course, have I realized that all of my worrying about something, was completely needless and a huge waste of my time? How many times in those many multiple times, was I correct about the amount of worrying being proportional to the circumstance?

Today I will create a 'Worry Meter' record and throughout my day, record the topic of worry which comes to mind and then rate it on a scale from 1-10. At day's end, I'll place my focus on the top three ratings so that I can confirm for myself the seriousness of my worry. I look forward to seeing which worries lose their rating, which ones slip away, and which ones are nothing more than me simply being responsible.

A Thought to Ponder at Dusk

Making a living has created a quality of living that has been consistent with the belief that I have about me. Having access to the appropriate amount of money is then what supports the quality and kind of living that I've chosen.

This has nothing to do with money and all to do with who I am and how I hold myself. Some of us feel that we need to work hard for a living and then there are some wealthy, privileged, and ultra-rich folks, who feel that working hard for a living is not in their DNA, yet they agree that others should work hard for them too.

A Thought to Ponder at Dawn

Nature has designed life and death to remain in a continuous flow.

To enjoy being in the easiest flow down the stream of my life, I will give up swimming and ride on the inner tube.

This vantage point gives *going with the flow* new meaning and opens realities that I never thought were possible.

A Thought to Ponder at Dusk

Who I am is a direct result of the quality of all my communications and my inner thoughts.

Whether I'm aware of it or not, the outcome doesn't just happen by accident, it's a habitual repetitive practice of consistent thoughts and communication.

Think and speak about new things and shift into a different quality of living.

Day 256

A Thought to Ponder at Dawn

The formula for creating anything is:

Idea + Focused Intention + Action = Manifestation.

Synonymous with: Inspiration + Intelligence + Movement = Result.

A Thought to Ponder at Dusk

Being continually present without thought is being in Truth - the *isness*. The Truth has the opportunity to be embraced in a realm of awakened mindlessness because that's where it lives.

The *you*-man existence, however, lives mostly in realities that are filled with thought.

A Thought to Ponder at Dawn

No matter how open-minded or *out of the box* I believe I can think, I can come from my single perspective about the boundaries of that box.

My mind's potential to have multiple perspectives occurring simultaneously is certainly possible, but not necessarily easy.

An example of a simultaneous perspective might be a *bitter-sweet* reality such as being thrilled to see a child off to school and yet being deeply sad at the same time.

Bearing witness to these simultaneous occurrences will be the task of the day - being present with the expansiveness of my mind's consciousness can open the doorway to a new realm of thinking.

A Thought to Ponder at Dusk

Gandhi was right when he said, "Be the change that you wish to see.", and here's why - Only I can envision and be that which I wish to see in my world and therefore the world because I *am* the source of my entire world.

A Thought to Ponder at Dawn

Without the mind, there are no thoughts, no awareness to relate to, and no reality to live inside of.

Without exception, my mind creates everything that I think and believe.

Never once has my mind ever failed at this task.

A Thought to Ponder at Dusk

My mind is sometimes awake because of me, while other times it's fast asleep.

Aware of it or not, my mind is always running the show and gives meaning to everything that it sees and does.

The longer it remains awake, the sooner it will come to know *me* and the more blissful life it will have.

A Thought to Ponder at Dawn

My eyes see the beautiful *spirit* in others when they are clear from whatever is blinding them.

I alone am responsible for having a clear vision.

Anything less than seeing anyone as beautiful in some manner is a smear on my lenses.

A Thought to Ponder at Dusk

Mindfulness is a lifetime practice of many things, one of which is remaining awake to the amazing mortal relationship between my mind and my body.

Where I go from there is on to a place that only my imagination can take me now and remains to be realized.

A Thought to Ponder at Dawn

When my mind realizes that I am the *spirit*, it bows in gratitude and service.

I don't have a job or anything to do; simply *being* the *light* allows my mind to eventually come around when it's ready.

A Thought to Ponder at Dusk

Language is a beautiful, limited method of communication that assimilates collectively agreed-upon words to interpret the perception of experiences.

More easily said, language is a way to share stuff that is all made up.

All of the made-up stuff is quite real, often significant, certainly meaningful, at times very impactful, and is most often camouflaged and sold off as truth… be mindful because it is never that.

A Thought to Ponder at Dawn

Our existence doesn't mean anything until you and I make it mean something.

Living a life with created passion and purpose is synonymous with living a life of joy and abundance.

A Thought to Ponder at Dusk

Being the *I am* that *I am,* is fine although often viewed as rather insignificant and noncontributory in my *you*-man experience.

The degree of impact of this awareness has shown up when my mind realizes how much better off it is when it sees and creates its interpretations while having the lights on.

Creating life in darkness is often a real crap shoot.

A Thought to Ponder at Dawn

Realizing that I am neither my mind nor body, poses the question, 'Who or what am I?'

The answer? I am that which illuminates my mind to ask the question.

What would a day in the life of my mind look like if I were able to remain awake to this throughout my day... throughout my week... throughout my life?

A Thought to Ponder at Dusk

Language both coins and limits reality, but it's all I've got ... or is it?

Meditation grants me the doorway to another realm of reality, one which is expanded and allows my reality to be filled with limitless possibilities.

Although meditation is not a place where words are spoken, it allows for thoughtlessness which is certainly a place where infinite energy swishes and swirls; aren't thoughts nothing more than manifested energy?

A Thought to Ponder at Dawn

Through devoted meditation practice, my mind can stop thinking and simply just listen.

It is then able to take clear and concise dictation from infinite intelligence - that which is on the *other side*.

The exercise I've taken on in having conversations with God has clearly illustrated this for me and allowed me to recognize the point where my thoughts end and others are being dictated in.

This is a beautiful way to clear my mind and allow greater consciousness to be my minister.

A Thought to Ponder at Dusk

A breakdown becomes a breakthrough when I surrender and release the stronghold and resistance that I have on my interpretation of an experience.

What am I willing to admit I am still *white-knuckled* about and ready to be freed from?

A Thought to Ponder at Dawn

Being mindful to allow and accept my interpretation about a person, place, or thing makes the powerful and passive process of transformation possible because only when I can see what I've created, am I allowed to choose whether it's worth keeping or not.

A Thought to Ponder at Dusk

Sustaining a transformed life is possible when my mind is consistently balanced and non-reactive, regardless of daily circumstances; it doesn't get any better than that for now.

A Thought to Ponder at Dawn

Being mindful of the outside world and knowing that everyone and everything is a mirrored reflection of my interpretations, is a direct confirmation that reality can only exist inside my mind.

A Thought to Ponder at Dusk

The onset of my identity was a funny gag gift that was inherited from dead ancestors.

Then, not to make matters worse, I adopted add-ons from the living family members after I was born and took on some more identity training in school and community.

I've never been without an identity, nor do I know what it's like not to have one.

Perhaps one day I will.

Until then, I can dream of what life would look like if I didn't have all of the training to be this persona that I never asked for — not like it's a bad thing either.

A Thought to Ponder at Dawn

A spiritual master is both engaged and detached from their identity and also non-reactive and indifferent to opinion, allowing them to embrace what heaven on earth would look like.

A Thought to Ponder at Dusk

Integrity is the awakened state of being in synchronicity with my words and my deeds.

It takes integrity to be in integrity.

A Thought to Ponder at Dawn

Feeling alone is an illusion of separation which tends to produce fear and instability.

This unbalanced state often throws the identity into survival mode.

The dysfunctional behavior and action which follows are credible as well as validated by those past interpretations.

Loving thoughts allow kindness, compassion, and forgiveness, to diminish and neutralize fear.

A Thought to Ponder at Dusk

Being upset about anything, whether it's a large or a small issue, is the *telltale* sign of proof needed to confirm that hidden *truth* is lurking somewhere inside of my mind's *thoughtmosphere* - the space where thoughts live - which needs to be spotlighted and examined.

Once uncovered and acknowledged for the valid *belief* that it is, I'm able to responsibly choose to create another point of view that serves and nourishes my growth and happiness.

A Thought to Ponder at Dawn

It takes integrity to have integrity.

Whether spoken or written, it sometimes takes conscious effort to honor the words that I communicate along with the power and impact that they have on others.

Self-integrity is the act of holding myself responsible for what I say and do. Being consistent in behavior to the words that I speak, is proof enough for me that I have my integrity in place.

With integrity, workability is made possible.

A Thought to Ponder at Dusk

My mind creates all of my reality's illusions. To hold a blind eye to this vantage point sets me up for many devastating challenges.

Being responsible for everything I think, feel, and say, prevents me from being a victim of circumstance and allows me the freedom of new choices at any moment.

Whenever I look at what ails me from this vantage point, I hold a master key to happiness and freedom.

A Thought to Ponder at Dawn

It's time to rebrand the word, 'selfishness' into a positive and essential word that represents health and well-being. What better word to use to honor and care for me and be most proud of, than the word, selfish?

When I honor myself and am not nice to someone or something, that's not selfish at all, it's mean and unkind. I place integrity back into the behavior which honors myself in any way that I can muster and will teach others how awesome it is to be selfish while still being considerate, kind, caring, and loving. This invite will go out to all of those whom I know can use a little 'to me - from me', gift.

A Thought to Ponder at Dusk

When I allow my mind to take charge, *I - spirit -* am its prisoner for life. I am committed to breaking away from the many years of my mind's reign of dictatorship.

Expanding my reality into one which serves, honors, and allows me to have a life that I love, takes awareness, courage, and the will to obliterate every bit of my current 'B'elief 'S'ystem that continues to hold any embedded truth.

When I realize that my autobiography is identical to a fiction novel, I'll be free to create the next chapters of my life consciously and purposefully.

A Thought to Ponder at Dawn

Without any interpretation of me, whether my own or anyone else's, my existence would have little, if no meaning whatsoever.

What this means is that I am a summation of collective interpretations.

Some of the ones which bind me are from my familial elders, who did their best to teach me all that they knew.

I begin to understand the cycle of life more clearly when I realize that the passing of the baton was passed down from all of those beloved elders and was also made up of a massive collection of interpretations.

I will embrace my life with more understanding and compassion for not having seen this sooner and assure myself that any self-interpretation comes from a place of forwarding my health and well-being.

A Thought to Ponder at Dusk

There is something more rare than unrealized talent, it's the ability to recognize unrealized talent.

As I close my eyes and breathe, I look within to recall a talent that I have that is not yet realized.

A Thought to Ponder at Dawn

You can't fix your reality, but you can certainly *enlighten* it.

The simple reason is that there is nothing whatsoever to be fixed, only seen.

This dysfunctional and broken vantage point has plagued humanity for millennia as a collective and grossly incorrect belief that continues to exist inside of a global reality-based illusion.

The kind of freedom to create around this vantage point right now, is similar to the awareness of an eagle who was told that it couldn't fly, only to realize that it could because it was born to do just that.

A Thought to Ponder at Dusk

A bird who is in search of twigs for its nest or seeking worms for food is laser-focused and very intentional.

Unlike us, most animals including birds remain conscious in every waking moment.

They have also learned to sleep much lighter than humans, which hasn't seemed to impinge on their stamina.

A Thought to Ponder at Dawn

A tree, a toad, and a sparrow are clueless about who they are.

Interestingly enough, the tree knows to stand tall and spread its branches, the sparrow knows to nest in its branches, and the toad knows to burrow under the fallen leaves.

Innate behavior such as this mirrors inner wisdom. Like most human beings, I have given up much of my natural instincts to live in society, away from nature.

Perhaps it's time to put a little organic environment back into my life.

A Thought to Ponder at Dusk

Sometimes an expression of love for someone is to simply offer up a new perspective before agreeing to respect their request to be and do as they please.

I know that whenever I have more options, it's easier to see the healthiest choice. Helping others to see the possibility of their choices oftentimes can make all the difference.

The challenge is to learn a way of communication that occurs as loving and compassionate.

A Thought to Ponder at Dawn

I experience countless things and yet I can only live inside of my interpretations of them.

An experience itself, is the is-ness or vibrational *truth* of someone or something, while my interpretation is my reality of it.

The *truth* is instantly taken out of every experience to find a way to relate to it and then share it with others. This is because everyone and everything is simply their own *is-ness*, to which there is no differentiation in which to relate.

To relate inside of my human experience, I must collectively agree to the particular interpretations about people, places, and things, to belong and fit in. As a side note, people who understand collective interpretations and yet don't agree with them, often find themselves not fitting in.

A Thought to Ponder at Dusk

Behaving in a manner that is consistently loving, kind, compassionate, and free, opens the doorway to heaven on earth. There will always be the concept of what I understand as evil while I live in a human experience.

The reality of good and evil will end when I take my final exhale. This will allow me to exist inside the *true* form of unconditional love — the full acceptance and allowance of *all that is* and *all that is not* — for all of eternity.

A Thought to Ponder at Dawn

Awareness is when consciousness turns the lights on and allows my mind to see itself with clarity.

The challenge of a lifetime is to hold myself accountable as the generator who keeps the lights on.

A Thought to Ponder at Dusk

A collective agreement stating that something is correct, doesn't make it righter or even true, for that matter.

Forgetting that I live in a world of agreement, directly influences, and oftentimes hinders my ideas on what is possible.

I will be mindful that whatever I agree to, will be right, and yet never righter than someone else's agreement, and certainly be never truer.

A Thought to Ponder at Dawn

When my mind can perceive and interpret something, that thing then becomes real.

This underscores my responsibility and accountability for creating my own reality.

A Thought to Ponder at Dusk

Self-realization is the awareness that sets me upon *you*-mankind's final frontier.

My interest and focus on understanding what's involved in the process of self-realization only makes me want to do whatever is required and behave in a manner that is consistent with my creation of it.

A Thought to Ponder at Dawn

Being mindful to fully accept everything for being just as it is, contributes to having a more comprehensive understanding that nothing ever *needs* to be fixed.

This doesn't however mean that fixing things isn't appropriate, as a matter of fact, it very well can be.

The distinction here is that the energy behind the *having to be* fixed is where the issues are often generated. That underlying energetic impetus is often toxic or unkind to the body and without it, there's so much more freedom and ease in creating something new.

I will stop fixing myself from this moment forward and notice the amount of freedom and ease I can muster.

A Thought to Ponder at Dusk

When someone wishes me good luck, it sometimes pulls my focus away from acknowledging my ability as reason enough for why I am successful.

When I wish others my 'good intentions' instead, however, it helps them refocus their awareness to be mindful of their abilities.

A Thought to Ponder at Dawn

When my mind recognizes *me* as the *spirit* within, it accepts and welcomes *me* as a priceless contribution to its continued creation of healthier and happier realities.

I will *lighten up* my mind today and watch when it checks in with itself to see how it's doing inside of the reality it's created.

A Thought to Ponder at Dusk

My mind is an *insistent interpreter* of all that it perceives and continually collects organic sensory data which is provided by my brain.

All the while *I* exist as I am and witness when my mind uses my light to be more mindful.

When I intentionally close my eyes, my mind can look into the vast darkness and simultaneously use its awareness to scan deeply inside of my human body and realize where *I* claim temporary residence.

A Thought to Ponder at Dawn

The potential for self-realization is a miraculous gift available to everyone.

With this gift of enlightenment comes the challenge of living in unwavering mindfulness.

When I assimilate today's intentions of gratitude, peace, and love, into my physiology, I will be committed to remaining aware of them and the goodness they generate.

A Thought to Ponder at Dusk

One of life's most challenging realities is to recognize the persistent illusions which masquerade as absolute truth. History is defined as the period between the beginning of time and now.

This means that the moment a thought becomes conscious, whether spoken or not, it instantly becomes part of the past. The generation of anything, including thought, as well as the state of awakened consciousness itself, is always in the present moment.

Interestingly enough, the acknowledgment and interpretation of thoughts quickly shift into the past as well. Except for meditation, or any activity where being in the moment is the primary focus, much of my daily life is lived in the immediate past.

A Thought to Ponder at Dawn

Normal recognition of thought often means that it has already been created. When my thoughts are being created, they occur in the now. There is an *energy* present just before that thought which allows its generation.

In a matter of a minute, if I'm quiet, mindful, and focused, I can close my eyes and witness my thinking process in action. Once I see this, I'll notice my face smiling at this new perspective and be able to take this into my day.

I also want to acknowledge that I may not have had those thoughts, but rather just simply watched them come to mind.

A Thought to Ponder at Dusk

The more that I go in search of *truth* inside of reality, the more down the rabbit hole of illusion I plummet.

All attempts will fail because I'm looking from the realm of reality and all that is real.

To know the *truth* outside of what is real is to first be mindless.

This occurs both with deeply devotional meditation and when I take my final exhale.

A Thought to Ponder at Dawn

Today, I will be mindful not to allow my mind's evidence from yesterday's news, to take up too much of today's current events.

Failing at this challenge will only serve to help remind me to further pay attention to what I say and do.

I will Capré Diem with Wonder and Joy!

A Thought to Ponder at Dusk

An Anytime Prayer For Anyone

God, Jesus, Mother Earth, Infinite Intelligence, and Saints of All Religions,

Help me to understand how to live with a more expanding heart and mind, create a playing field for clearer intuition, and give more attention to my body's shifts in sensations as a way of direct communication.

My heart and mind recognize and celebrate the blessings that I, *spirit*, bring to the human experience. With devoted practice, my trust and faith deepen. I enter a sacred space, embrace my fears, become love itself, and live freely inside of the balanced circle of life.

A Thought to Ponder at Dawn

Knowledge is information that I've placed an agreement upon and then held to account over the years, I hold on to this data until something new comes along to either disprove it or expand upon it.

I understand this when I look for instance, at all of the advancements made in transportation from the beginning of mankind until now. It's a more difficult task when it regards looking at my lifespan, from what beliefs I've inherited, then adapted to those which I've perpetuated.

To find any freedom around who and what I am, I must realize that all the knowledge I hold about myself, and even others for that matter, has been created and then fabricated into stories of proclamation and agreement. Knowing this allows me to either choose to continue and build upon my biographical story or create another chapter in my novel from scratch, simply because it moves me.

A Thought to Ponder at Dusk

Communication is my mind's masterful way to learn, understand, interpret, and gain agreement, within my reality. One of the greatest ironies and pitfalls is that although my senses tell me that there is an *out there* which exists outside of my mind and body, there is no such thing.

Not only is it all very real, but it is also rather easy to gain agreement that there is an *out there*. The *out there* which perceive exists only inside of my mind.

A Thought to Ponder at Dawn

Whether I'm looking to figure out how to make an amazing spaghetti sauce or seeking to understand the nature of a brand-new solar system in the cosmos, every speck of reality is interpreted inside of my mind.

What this means for me is that I'm fully responsible for everything I believe and don't believe.

I'm also accountable for when I hold onto old beliefs that are harmful to my health and well-being. Off the top of my head, I can recall some of these beliefs and will jot them down and explore why they still linger when I know they are not *true*.

A Thought to Ponder at Dusk

One of the biggest challenges to mindful living is knowing that I am always exactly right where I need to be at all times.

Whenever I'm upset about something, realizing this provides me with an instant reset in thought and allows me to approach things from a more empowered perspective.

A Thought to Ponder at Dawn

Whenever I stop and take just a small chain of *now* moments to be in stillness and quiet, I gain a glimpse of eternity.

By giving the word, *eternity*, a meaning of infinite and unending, it's fair to say that I am currently living in eternity.

From this vantage point, although I'm unable to fully grasp how old I am, I realize that my time on earth as a human being is shorter than a nanosecond about how long eternity goes on.

A Thought to Ponder at Dusk

An 'old soul' is a conjured-up term that allows my mind and body to recognize *me* as a *being* who has come back to enjoy another enriching human experience.

It also infers that in some manner, I'm a bit wiser than the average soul. The interesting thing is that there is even an average soul. Hmmm.

A Thought to Ponder at Dawn

Until we showed up on earth about two million years ago, life on our planet had no way of being interpreted and the universe had no existence.

Neither a tree nor a frog has any idea that they are a tree or a frog, the universe is clueless as well.

The only place that the universe exists is solely in my mind.

For anything to have an existence, there must be a cognitive way of relating to it.

So too is my temporary life on earth - my life exists because of you and me and I am grateful.

A Thought to Ponder at Dusk

Time and space are a couple of our greatest illusions and like the sea that fish swim in, it goes unnoticed while powerfully influencing our whereabouts.

When I'm asleep in dreamland, time and space either vanish or are often grossly distorted in some manner.

My sleep state is a more accurate account of what my world will be like in years to come.

A Thought to Ponder at Dawn

During archery practice, the Greeks had created the word, *sin*, to mean missing the mark.

It was a sin when the mark was missed.

The Christians then borrowed the term and taught us that just by being human, we all missed the mark.

Would it have been God's sin to have created mankind?
Just something to respectfully ponder.

A Thought to Ponder at Dusk

What are memories other than a benchmark that we were here or validation of our existence?

The many years of picture taking, videos, and retelling of stories allow me to feel the joys and comforts of my life.

Compared to the past, my unknown future can leave me a bit anxious. However, being conscious of my present moments confirms that I am right where I need to be and allows me to easily embrace my center of power.

A Thought to Ponder at Dawn

There have been countless times in my life when I've fibbed and retold stories without 100% accuracy. The telling of alternative facts is a mark against my integrity because I was conscious of having altered the tale.

In addition, when I'm representing a story accurately and on point, I will still have a mark against my integrity if I'm attempting to share it like it's true, especially when I know that everything in my mind is all made up. A powerful mind is fully responsible and accountable for everything that it creates because it knows that it created it. I promised myself and others to never lie and never tell the truth either, simply because it's not possible. The only thing I can do is share my perspective.

A Thought to Ponder at Dusk

An open mind is an expanding and scientific mind because it looks at things from a place of inquiry, wonder, and discovery, instead of going in search of results.

The state of deep sleep is a perfect realm to play with my discovery. Before going into slumber each night, placing a laser focus on my inhale and exhale, takes me out of time and space as I slide deeply into uncharted territory.

My other challenge is placing focus on remembering what happened while I was on the other side. Being quiet, still, fully relaxed, and calm, my recall is pretty telling.

A Thought to Ponder at Dawn

When the illusion of any hidden truth is uncovered and brought to light, that truth quickly vanishes when reality sets in.

This is always a perfect opportunity to be responsible and create my own reality.

What can I make up about how today is going to go and make sure that it goes as planned?

A Thought to Ponder at Dusk

A normal mind says: 'When everything is well, I will be happy.'

An enlightened mind says: 'When I choose happiness, all is well.'

A Thought to Ponder at Dawn

The act of observing with indifference allows an awakened mind to be fully engaged, detached, and present.

In addition, being non-reactive to people, places, or circumstances, is my greatest challenge which will yield my greatest joy.

Taking this on as a mindful practice with the awareness that the quality of my life depends upon it, will allow me to encounter what people call, 'heaven on earth'.

A Thought to Ponder at Dusk

Even though I know how old I am, what age do I physically, psychologically, and emotionally feel that I am?

I will close my eyes before falling asleep and recall a favorite childhood memory.

Giving myself only 15-20 minutes of remembrance will begin to alter my physiology.

Although taking this on as a serious and daily meditative practice won't make me any younger, it will noticeably impact my health and energy levels

Day 289

A Thought to Ponder at Dawn

Transformational moments always occur in the *now* and result in greater clarity and understanding.

What am I unclear about right now that needs some light of awareness?

I honor my mind whether clear or not and continue to shed light on areas that still challenge me.

A Thought to Ponder at Dusk

Although my mind thinks in present moments, it's not usually present in the particular moments that it's thinking in, unless, of course, it's having an Ah-Ha Moment.

Ah-ha moments are precious and usually occur when we least expect them. I challenge myself to close my eyes and recall the mental feelings and physical sensations of a particular Ah-Ha moment without any of the associated details.

Doing so diligently can alter my physiology just as if I was having an Ah-Ha moment right now.

This reinforces the awareness of my ability to create and alter my physiology on a cellular level and in a positive manner, and also makes it appealing to commit to a daily practice of visualization

Day 290

A Thought to Ponder at Dawn

Thinking from a completely new perspective requires will and persistence because of the challenge to sustain thoughts that are new and unfamiliar, as opposed to any dysfunctional comfort of the familiar.

The big advantage of behaving in this manner is the inspiration to generate new realities that otherwise would never have been made possible.

A Thought to Ponder at Dusk

When my mind is present, it is often quiet.

When my mind is thinking, it is often filled with noise.

Living in a balanced state of mind allows my body to be healthy and allows me to enjoy the quality and integrity of a life being well lived.

Therefore each night, I will empty the lingering trash of thoughts from my mind and allow beautiful space to appear for a deeper and regenerative slumber.

A Thought to Ponder at Dawn

Being mindful allows me to realize that everything that I think and believe is a *truth-less* reality that blesses me with the option of powerfully choosing a new perspective from an infinite realm of reality.

The absence of *truth* is the key that unlocks the door to all that is possible.

A Thought to Ponder at Dusk

Before an assigned word with any associated meaning is given to something or someone, it holds little value or significance.

As a newborn, I can only imagine how beautiful my white canvas must have been before my significant caregivers gave me an identity along with their beliefs and interpretations of their world.

When I think about who I am and what I'm able to create for myself, it opens up a world of wonder, exploration, excitement, and passion to create myself.

A Thought to Ponder at Dawn

There is no way to relate to anything until I either make it all up or learn what the interpretation is that was made up by others.

Being mindful of this allows me to create my daily living to be as extraordinary as I wish it to be, especially when I'm present to the greater unknown.

A Thought to Ponder at Dusk

To allow any fear of the inevitable, like fearing death, to have any power over me, is a waste of energy and precious time, all of which, will never be reimbursed.

What can it hurt if I decided to focus on all that is good and rebuke, disallow, and trash, any negative thought that enters my mind from now on?

Nada is the answer.

I release each negative thought into the vast trash barrel of the universe, knowing that it will be recycled and reabsorbed.

A Thought to Ponder at Dawn

A breakdown vanishes when I forfeit a made-up *truth* about something and take full responsibility for having misinterpreted the perspective that had rendered me powerless.

A Thought to Ponder at Dusk

When I recall the people I've come into contact with today, I can see each of them in my mind and witness their perspectives and realities and how they are all different from one another.

However, the amazing thing is that although they all have their own vantage points which are just as unique as mine, we are all *unique* just like everyone else.

I can now fall into a deep slumber and embrace my mind around the oneness of us all.

A Thought to Ponder at Dawn

What I'd like to create today for myself is: _____
_____.

What I'd like to create today for others is: _____
_____.

What I am grateful for today is: _____
_____.

What I'll be bringing to bed with me this evening is the joy from a day of fulfilled wants and desires. Should I not have met my mark, there will be another opportunity tomorrow.

A Thought to Ponder at Dusk

Instead of looking for love any further, I stop now to examine and embrace the internal blocks of proof for why I am holding myself back from simply *being* the love I seek in the first place.

A Thought to Ponder at Dawn

When my interpretation of an experience becomes the *way it is*, truth is deeply embedded into that reality and the power of free expression and validation of any other vantage point is lost.

As I go through my day, I will uncover my hidden truths every time I feel a loss of power and expression. This is a welcomed challenge required for my freedom and self-realization.

A Thought to Ponder at Dusk

Reality is right, valid, meaningful, real, significant, and yet is Never *true*. An example of this would be if I called a monkey a, "monkey," straight to their face, and then they looked at me strangely and said, "What on earth are you talking about!?" (Providing monkeys can talk!)

I'd be completely right in my vantage point, and so validated if others agreed with me. The monkey, however, probably has their take on who they are which is just as right as my perspective.

And if that monkey happened to come from the planet of the apes, they'd think all human beings are beneath them in the food chain. That would be just as right as me calling them a monkey.

A Thought to Ponder at Dawn

Buddha's message on love which is to open our hearts is clear, scientific, and immediately applicable.

What makes love such a powerful energetic vibration, is its universal blanketing of allowance and acceptance.

Compassion, joy, and equanimity, along with love, make up the very nature of a self-realized individual.

Being a host to these traits is a blessing and even more so when I see that they are still there at the end of the day.

A Thought to Ponder at Dusk

I am aware of being mindful when my mind sees itself thinking and observing.

Enlightenment comes to mind the moment it knows that *I am* the light.

Knowing this and being this is not the same. Being this requires me to get quiet, still, breathe, and watch with devotion and patience.

A Thought to Ponder at Dawn

For my mind to accept and embrace *me* (*spirit*) living inside of a physical body, is to know the *me* which resides inside of every living being that has a heartbeat.

It is in the illusion of separation that the concept of oneness is addressed to remind us that physical structures are never a barrier.

No physical body or concrete wall can separate that which is omnipresent.

A Thought to Ponder at Dusk

An authentic practice of self-love includes accepting and allowing my thinking to be exactly where it is.

It also includes me visiting the realm of thoughtlessness as well, to cleanse and rejuvenate my mind.

A Thought to Ponder at Dawn

For every cause, there is an effect, and for every action, a reaction. Causes and actions are constituents of creation itself, both of which have no claim or interest in any of the outcomes.

Creation, as in the Big Bang which created a solar system, had no vested interest in what the outcome would look like. This is very different from creating something out of a need, want, or desire; they all have an interest in the outcome.

Clearly stated, authentic creation is generated from nothing.

A Thought to Ponder at Dusk

If God is the Creator, it is then accurate to say that God is the un-manifestation of that which has yet to manifest.

The key is to understand that once something is made manifest, it is *of* God and is *not* God itself.

I am an energetic being that has been created from this unimaginable 'un-manifested source.

Similar to fractal mathematics, my ability to create from *nothingness*, is God in action. The focus now is to explore what nothingness is. I can take that one to my dream state.

A Thought to Ponder at Dawn

The magnitude and intensity of any upset resulting from failed expectations are directly proportional to the energetic investment I have in it.

The magnitude and intensity of all joy that stems from exceeding expectations are directly proportional to the energetic investment I have made in it.

Bottom line? - I will invest wisely.

A Thought to Ponder at Dusk

At first, the young, empty mind, with wonder and excitement, gathers as much information as it can to learn all about life and figure things out.

The old mind, however, is often a full mind which seeks to clear as much of the clutter, that it can enjoy the emptiness of a young mind.

My devoted meditation practice allows me to be familiar with thoughtlessness which brings inner peace, calm, and joy while restoring balance in my days.

A Thought to Ponder at Dawn

One of the greatest secrets of life is to be completely ok when things are not ok with me.

Another big secret is to allow me to not be ok with not being ok.

The greatest freedom in life, however, is to allow me to be wherever I am in my life.

The freedom to be comfortable in which ever-changing mindset I happen to be in, at any given moment, allows me to flow with life itself.

A Thought to Ponder at Dusk

There are three ways in which to view my world.

Choosing a *negative* view is just as *untrue* as me choosing a *positive* one, both of which still yield relatively predictable results.

Choosing *indifference* as a third view, although considered spiritually enlightened, is also *untrue,* and yet offers a deep and unbridled sense of freedom and happiness.

A Thought to Ponder at Dawn

An over-crowded mind can short-circuit itself.

A busy mind is filled with interpretations.

A quiet mind is calm and peaceful.

An empty mind opens the door to heaven on earth.

I meditate to clear, renew, and rejuvenate my mind.

I create my day each morning by setting my focus and intentions in a direction and then will accept and allow whatever comes.

A Thought to Ponder at Dusk

The awareness of everything being just *as it is*, realizing that whatever meaning is then given to it, is fictitious at best, acknowledges the existence of the experience itself, as pure.

All experiences are pure; it is my interpretation of them that adds meaning, which then voids the truth.

The truth lies in the *is-ness*, never in the interpretation.

A Thought to Ponder at Dawn

Turning my wrist inward, pointing my index finger towards myself, allows me to know who's responsible for creating the only world I have ever known.

The world that I live in exists only inside of my mind.

A Thought to Ponder at Dusk

Having a tight hold on my interpretations paralyzes any possibility of creating new perspectives and seals off access to freedom and happiness.

Whatever I resist giving up, will own me until I do.

A Thought to Ponder at Dawn

An experience is an energetic occurrence that my mind then interprets into a perspective.

It's kind of obsolete to say that I ever have an experience, when in fact I always create an interpretation about an experience and then make the mistake of calling it an experience.

Being responsible for the creation of my interpretation allows it to be as valid as anyone else's.

An experience is the same for everyone, it's the interpretation that is different.

A Thought to Ponder at Dusk

This is the key to healing and transformation.

It's impossible to change or erase any experience which has already occurred, nor would anyone want to.

By changing the perspective of an experience, I open the doorway to the world of transformation.

A Thought to Ponder at Dawn

When my will is motivated by my ego, I have the power to manifest all that is real.

My conscious connection to the infinite allows my will to become Thy Will and manifest all that is good.

When I quiet the chatter in my mind and focus on thy will, I know exactly how to move forward in service.

A Thought to Ponder at Dusk

Reality is deceptive - it can be deceptively beautiful, deceptively horrifying, or just deceptively benign, depending on the chosen vantage point of preference.

As Dr. Einstein said, 'Reality is an illusion, albeit a persistent one.' Approaching life's circumstances with an open mind allows me to create my own game of life.

Although many serious life challenges don't usually feel like a game, there's always wiggle room to give me permission to impart some fun and play into every approach.

A Thought to Ponder at Dawn

I hold no distinction between fiction and nonfiction.

Living in a world of illusion, I substitute *truth* with a*uthentic reality*, which is the best that I or anyone can do.

This allows for the infinite possibility to be available when choosing to believe whatever feeds and nourishes my mind, body, and spirit.

My ability to sustain this shift in awareness till my last exhale is the challenge of my lifetime, so I'll begin now.

A Thought to Ponder at Dusk

My mind uses cognitive knowledge as an effective default to remain comfortable within the illusion of safety, homeostasis, and stability.

Knowing that's not *true*, what would my life look like if I surrendered to that reality?

A Thought to Ponder at Dawn

Knowing that my legacy will be based on people's interpretations of me, places me at a crossroads.

I can spend the rest of my life doing and saying things that people want to hear, just for their approval and applause, or I can express who I am by living from my heart, trusting my gut, and doing my best to teach others by example while paying little attention to what they may conjure up about me.

One way is extremely exhausting to even think about, let alone try to execute, while the other choice is the way of the Freedom Warrior.

A Thought to Ponder at Dusk

The scientific understanding of cosmic balance is achieved by going beyond the perception of chaos, and recognizing that over many trillions of years, there is in fact, universal order.

My entire world begins and ends inside of my mind and is with a collective agreement that I exist as an identity.

The gestation period in my mother's womb is a representational microcosm of how the chaos of how just two cells can divide and multiply into millions and billions and then differentiate into the specialized matter, bringing complete order to my human form.

A Thought to Ponder at Dawn

Looking through the eyes of inquiry and wonder is a foundation for clean discoveries.

Learning and mastering a particular subject matter increases the risk of losing one's pair of inquiring eyes and therefore is important to remain mindful.

A beautiful daily practice is to focus on each moment and every day being brand new.

A Thought to Ponder at Dusk

A friend is like a treasured gemstone, not easy to find and impossible to replace. Although we hear that most people can count their real friends on just one hand, wouldn't it be a blessing to have lost count passed all of one's fingers and toes?

It is more important for me to like my friends than it is to love them. Loving them is easy while liking them requires compatibility and workability. This can be the most challenging.

This is the main reason why I cherish trusted friends as my chosen family. Taking the time to recall each of them warms my heart like a nice cup of cocoa.

A Thought to Ponder at Dawn

The interpretation that I give to a feeling, or an emotion directly influences my behavior and how I relate with others.

Thoughts and feelings which are habitual determine how my physical world, which includes my body, responds to me.

Mindfulness is needed to regulate the quality of my life.

A Thought to Ponder at Dusk

Whether it is internal or external, I am a product of my environment.

The most obvious reason is that I was born out of my environment which happens to go far beyond what my mind can even grasp.

Every atom, particle, molecule, and energetic vibration had its chance to create me. Everything that my parents are (were) and my grandparents are (were) and so on, contributed to me; and every atom, particle, molecule, etc., contributed to them as well and was recycled back after they left their bodies.

There is no separation between everyone and everything period, yet I live inside of the illusion that there is… silly me.

A Thought to Ponder at Dawn

Learning to be non-reactive with my thoughts while remaining respectful of a particular feeling or emotion, unleashes freedom and independence from an old, imprisoned relationship with myself.

Being non-reactive is a huge achievement that requires devotional practice and can simultaneously include achieving a state of indifference as a way of claiming a witnessing observer's position.

A Thought to Ponder at Dusk

Feelings of both pain and pleasure are two components that are sometimes intrinsic in one's act of loving someone or something, yet for the enlightened being, there is only a solid bounty of love with little or no upset.

A Thought to Ponder at Dawn

I AM that I AM - the *spirit*, the *witnessing observer*, the *light*, and the *way*, and my mind is what challenges my existence.

Enlightenment occurs when my mind bows to me in reverence.

A Thought to Ponder at Dusk

My spirit is the *cause* and *life* itself; my mind is the contract builder; my body, including all that is physical, is the outcome of the efforts of my mind.

I am the spirit that enlightens my mind when it's ready for an awakening.

Every thought that my mind holds has either been self-created or agreed upon.

Mind, body, and spirit are the companies of the human trilogy.

A Thought to Ponder at Dawn

It's been said that if I don't go within, I'll go without.

To live freely by engaging with outside illusions, however, I must first go within to realize that that's where the creation of all reality begins.

I create my reality which includes the world around me.

A Thought to Ponder at Dusk

Examining my mind objectively lets me see that there are many legitimate interpretations that I created specifically to protect my fears.

A few examples of this are creating an afterlife to comfort the fear of death or a loss of a loved one, feeling lucky to hit the lottery one day to camouflage a fear of never having financial freedom, and being skeptical and distrusting of others to comfort the fear of being lied to and deceived.

The repetitious perpetuation of thought serves to strengthen the reality of that particular belief. If not mindful, thoughts that are dysfunctional and toxic will remain until action is taken to create a new vantage point and again, practice strengthening it through repetition. Enlightenment is an awakened state of being non-reactive while remaining fully engaged with whatever is in front of me.

A Thought to Ponder at Dawn

I take on my day with love in my heart and the passion to make a difference for others.

Should I react negatively or positively, I will soon look at the cause and trigger of my response.

This is one of the tallest orders in spiritual growth and development, especially being non-reactive to positive things.

Gratitude and appreciation are separate and welcome and have nothing to do with reactivity.

A Thought to Ponder at Dusk

The human mind has been studied for many centuries and there are still so many unanswered questions about it.

Regardless of how much is known about it, it not only remains the reason for our existence but the quality of our life.

A healthy mind allows my body to flourish and so I focus on peace, calm, and health.

A Thought to Ponder at Dawn

On the occasions when I embrace a mindset of neutrality and indifference as a way of being, I become my own Buddha.

As a happy Buddha, I am clear of the silliness of my human mind.

A Thought to Ponder at Dusk

I am mindful that my feelings are quite real, full of meaning, and impact my entire life.

Whatever I choose to continually focus on and think about, will fill my days.

Since my environment plays a significant role in who I am, it is also wise for me to see what others are focusing on as well.

I remain mindful of selecting my environment as the gateway to the quality of life that I currently have.

A Thought to Ponder at Dawn

When I authentically share my feelings without having an agenda, they are an expressive reflection and indicator of where my present consciousness is.

Hidden agendas are trickier to spot yet. I can rely on my gut to tell me so.

Getting familiar with my awareness is key to knowing who and what I am.

A Thought to Ponder at Dusk

Interpretations are vantage points, focused thoughts of judgments, assessments, and evaluations, which are created about people, places, and things.

The mistake that I make is to ever think that agreements, collective or otherwise, are anything more than made up or fictitious.

This is my access to being happy and content in my self-created world.

A Thought to Ponder at Dawn

An awakened mind is a devoted servant and spirit companion because it recognizes *me* as the *light* and expression of *individual consciousness,* or whatever else I choose to call it that is neither my mind nor my body.

Although navigating throughout my day with this awareness might be atypical, doing so might open up a window for a new perspective.

A Thought to Ponder at Dusk

An enlightened mind knows the difference between needing to figure things out and seeking to understand, and no longer carries the burden of being driven by wants and needs.

A Thought to Ponder at Dawn

Three ways to live my life:

1. Hold people and situations responsible for my joys and woes.
2. Blame others and circumstances for why I'm challenged and take responsibility sometimes.
3. Be fully accountable for every perspective that I've created or agreed with for my life's quality.

I get to choose which vantage point to live from and receive the benefits/consequences of my choice.

A Thought to Ponder at Dusk

While meditation is the practice of mindlessness - it allows me to see the lingering chatter which occupies my mind's *thoughtmosphere*.

Meditating allows me to create empty mind space, which I can then choose to fill with more nourishing thoughts.

I can only achieve this through repetitive practice.

Day 317

A Thought to Ponder at Dawn

The key to having a solid meditation practice is to first acknowledge my thoughts and then let them be as they are while I refocus my attention on my breath.

Making meditation a lifetime practice is immensely rewarding and continues to fill my life with possibility.

A Thought to Ponder at Dusk

Everything about me that I've come to know is solely based on past events and circumstances that were both planned and unplanned.

If that's not enough, I was born with a mind whose purpose is to maintain order, keep the status quo, and continually create ways to understand to neutralize any fear of the unknown.

When I'm able to acknowledge having subconsciously written a great novel called, "My Life", I'm inspired to creatively write whatever I consciously choose.

A Thought to Ponder at Dawn

When my mind is *aware* of being in the moment, it's partly conscious of just being.

When I'm *in* an actual moment, no thoughts are infiltrating my mind. This occurs when I'm in deep meditation.

A Thought to Ponder at Dusk

It stands to reason that since my reality is a persistent illusion that never seems to go away, my identity, which is a key part of my reality, is also an illusion.

When I recall something about myself which is unpleasant or unappealing, I can now allow myself to transform into something worthwhile.

Also, when I think of people whom I've had an uneasy time with, I have the opportunity to alter my thoughts about them into something more worthwhile.

A Thought to Ponder at Dawn

Whenever my mind perceives a limitation, that itself is the limitation.

When my mind perceives possibility, that is the open door to all that is possible.

When I create my day, I am mindful to cast out any limitations and live my life in all that is possible.

A Thought to Ponder at Dusk

Every moment is a potential opportunity for me to create something new.

When I find myself stuck on something, I can instantly shift by recalling my ability to create whatever I choose.

Freedom and happiness show up to blanket me whenever I take on this mindset.

A Thought to Ponder at Dawn

The ability to understand and differentiate between the *absolute truth* and an authentic interpretation of what is real is a key to creating peace on earth.

To date, other than 'believing' in the *truth*, no one has yet to prove that the absolute *truth* exists in human reality; all that exists for me is my authentic interpretation of life.

If the *absolute truth* existed, we'd all have the same position, there would be only one true religion, not 3200 of them, and human reality would be vastly different and almost unrecognizable because there would only be one *true* way of doing things.

So in essence, the *absolute truth* takes away all individual expression of creativity.

A Thought to Ponder at Dusk

Psycholonics (psyche + colonics) - is a creative process of cleansing the psyche of unpleasant thinking. This process requires uncovering dysfunctional and unappealing thoughts and then watching them neutralize and disappear without doing anything to fix them.

Once aware of an upsetting thought, I realize that I can either remain the one responsible for continuing to feed that thought or watch it neutralize or vanish on its own. Simultaneously, I can choose to focus on happier and healthier thoughts.

A Thought to Ponder at Dawn

When I direct my focus on my breath at any moment, peace and calmness appear.

I will make this focal shift part of my repetitive daily practice especially when it comes to reducing stress and any upsets, great or small.

A Thought to Ponder at Dusk

An enlightened mind knows to look inward.

A sleeping mind looks to outside influences for just about everything including, but not limited to, self-worth, safety, love, acknowledgment, validation, approval, love, understanding, comfort, health, wealth, satisfaction, success, and on and on and on.

A mind that doesn't go within, goes with 'out'.

A Thought to Ponder at Dawn

A mind's gross misperception of being separate and alone is a cause and reason for creating the need for a path or a journey to go on to find belonging, acceptance, fellowship, and love.

It is important to underscore gross misperception because human eyes often base their opinions on what is seen instead of realizing that the impossibility of seeing all that is. As a *spirit, I am energy,* and energy is often felt and not seen.

My naked eyes can neither see what a microscope nor a telescope can see, which is proof of limited vision. It's important to remind myself to be humble in my approach to whatever I think when it comes from my eyesight.

A Thought to Ponder at Dusk

I create a proven and unwavering source of personal freedom and joy for myself when I hold no requirement for others to make that happen for me.

This is easy to understand and is made possible when I realize that everything I need is generated within my mind. When I've held others responsible for my happiness and liberty, I only faced temporary relief or disappointment for having given my power away.

Holding onto my power is important for the integrity and quality of my life.

A Thought to Ponder at Dawn

Confronting my fears is a perfect time to see them as the fictitious, hidden truths, which have kept them all in place.

My fear vanishes the moment that a particular untruth is exposed.

I will take a moment to start a list of all my fears and prioritize them in ascending order.

This will allow me to start small and prove to myself that meeting them is a great source of freedom and joy.

A Thought to Ponder at Dusk

My life and therefore reality is temporary.

Everything is temporary for that matter, except for what we collectively consider to be the absolute truth - if something is true, it can never be anything else.

So if by definition, the *absolute truth* is not a temporary occurrence, it's impossible to ever be a part of my reality.

Realizing this allows me to stand in whatever magnificent illusions that I so powerfully choose to create.

A Thought to Ponder at Dawn

The limitation of both my body's sensory organ systems and my mind's IQ limits my reality.

My ability to tap into greater consciousness, however, inspires my intuition to have access to something far greater than my own understanding.

When my mind is clear and receptive, I'm able to draw from this vast *thoughtmosphere*, of expanded consciousness and create an expanded reality.

I remain humbled knowing that until I transition back out of my body, I can find joy within the confines of my limitations.

A Thought to Ponder at Dusk

Every mind can differentiate between the inside and the outside world. An enlightened mind, however, knows that the outside world is only a reflection of illusive thoughts which it generates inside of itself.

A Thought to Ponder at Dawn

Today I make a concerted effort to wish as many people as possible that I come into contact with, whatever they may need.

Whether they need to find more peace. joy, health, freedom, happiness, abundance, etc, I will tell them that I wish them that *Always* and in *All Ways*.

To make sure that they fully understand the impact of my intention, I will look into their eyes and wait for their response.

A Thought to Ponder at Dusk

Mind mastery is a practice of remaining awake to observe not only what my mind is thinking, but why it might be thinking those particular thoughts.

The importance of this is for me to recognize and become comfortable with a shift in knowing who *I AM - I am* the *light* of the observation. When any action is taken, it is a result of my mind and not *me, the observer*.

A Thought to Ponder at Dawn

Being consistently awake and mindful helps me to realize that the heaven that we have conjured up, exists only on earth.

That which I think is heaven after I transition out of my body, there aren't words for. Anyone who has had a near-death experience and has gone out of their mind and body, had no eyesight, no sense of touch, smell, ability to speak, etc. at that time.

This is exactly the reason which explains whatever was thought to have happened, was created the moment they returned to their body and mind. Although hindsight is often considered to provide a much clearer perspective, in this case, interpreting what happened on the other side, is a feeble attempt to describe that which there are yet to be words.

A Thought to Ponder at Dusk

Being mindful of my capacity to love allows me to embrace another's reality as validly as my own and gives me access to a greater understanding of whom they've created themself to be.

A Thought to Ponder at Dawn

As my mind awakens, I begin to play with balance and neutrality and watch my need to fix anyone and anything, dissolve.

This is a sign of emancipation from a life-long fixated reality.

I create a day of awareness by allowing things that I already know, to occur as brand new and explore them as if it were my first time.

A Thought to Ponder at Dusk

Being mindful to create for me a beautiful pace and flow in life which is organic requires me to realize that what has stopped me is being more concerned with what others think of me.

That stops now as I close my eyes and tell all of those whom I love that there will be no more of this.

I will be mindful to love and accept everyone as they are and in doing so, will apply that intention to myself.

A Thought to Ponder at Dawn

The practice of meditation is ongoing, always deepening, and never something which can be mastered only expanded.

The practice of living in a human experience is ongoing, always expanding, and not something I will ever be able to master, so I might as well start by fully enjoying it and make that my constant way of being, no matter what.

A Thought to Ponder at Dusk

Mindfulness is a result of visualization and focused intentions which are backed by belief.

Mindlessness, on the other hand, is a result of meditation with a strong focus on the life force - the breath.

Mindfulness brings greater clarity and crispness to what is real, while mindlessness welcomes a vastness of space along with the notion that anything is possible.

A Thought to Ponder at Dawn

Influential beliefs which occurred during childhood and young adult life, the option to choose or to create my reality has always been mine to make.

Never realizing this back then, I just assumed that my reality about life itself, was pretty much set and done with, and all that I needed to do was learn how to accept it.

What a huge mistake that was!

Whenever I come across anyone who's struggling with something, I will attempt to be as kind as possible and help them to free themself by sharing this wisdom and in doing so, reinforce my power center.

A Thought to Ponder at Dusk

A new meaning for the word, **SELFISH**:

S - Serving *E* - Everyone *L* - Love, *F* - Furthers *I* - Increased *S* -Spiritual - *H* – Health

I allow *selfishness* to yield love and bring peace and calm into my world.

A Thought to Ponder at Dawn

One of the greatest challenges of the enlightenment-seeking process is to realize that there is nowhere else that is better to be than where I am, right now.

I will practice remembering this for as long as I remain forgetful.

A Thought to Ponder at Dusk

I am always already in the exact place where I belong.

It's impossible to be anywhere else.

An imbalance arises when there's confusion about this.

Remaining aware of this raises my level of contentment and satisfaction to be enough.

A Thought to Ponder at Dawn

Every thought has an associated energy which fuels its existence.

Consistently creating thoughts that are upsetting or uncomfortable, will continue to yield internal dis-ease.

I am mindful to create peace and happiness throughout my day and will watch for a more joyful and healthier me and who knows, I might find myself whistling or singing.

A Thought to Ponder at Dusk

Most actions that I take are a result of associated thoughts.

An exception to this would be closing my eyes while listening to music and allowing my body to move in a dance.

Here, no thought is required and it's all about movement and sound energy.

In daily living, however, what will life be like when I take complete charge of the thoughts that my mind thinks?

No matter what the outcome is, the responsibility for how it plays out is all mine.

A Thought to Ponder at Dawn

The brain is different from other organs because my mind uses it to navigate through life.

My life will be significantly different when I am no longer in service to my mind, but rather be its master.

Reality is mine for the choosing.

A Thought to Ponder at Dusk

Reflection is a gift that allows me to recall fond memories.

Any past sentiment that is felt from my reflection, recreates the same energetic vibration right now and can directly alter my physiology once more.

Knowing this makes me more mindful to reflect on memories that bring me joy.

Whenever a thought comes in that is unpleasant, I will forgive myself and return to fond memories.

I look forward to taking those vibrations into my sleep world.

A Thought to Ponder at Dawn

Individual consciousness — *spirit* — as we are oftentimes called, ignites our mind's awareness of life on earth. *We* enter into a temporal body causing the heart to take its first beat.

We hopefully live a rich life and then blissfully leave the earth suit upon our final exhale.

Cloaking a veil of forgetfulness over this expanded awareness helps us focus on the significant illusions of day-to-day living.

This behavior is commonplace and helps to generate a quality of life. Challenges that we face in life can be a gift to help us remember who we are and find a better balance during our time in a human experience.

A Thought to Ponder at Dusk

To play the game of life with complete freedom is to welcome the unknown as a trusted friend and allow my human life to organically transform without any help from me.

Getting out of the way allows the flow of life to continue without any interruption.

Once I have a *heart-to-heart* conversation, so to speak, with my mind, this can be made possible.

A Thought to Ponder at Dawn

The practice of Freedomization allows consciousness to expand through understanding.

For this to happen, I first become *aware* of a confronting thought.

Secondly, I welcome and *allow* it into my mind space because it's already there.

Finally, I place my focus and intention on *accepting* it, just the way it is.

I realize that nothing stays the same and when I accept and allow something to be, as it is, it transforms on its own, without any help from me, gifts me with so much more free time.

A Thought to Ponder at Dusk

Inside of every present moment exists a blissfulness and a sense of freedom, which has no relative opposite.

Although precious moments aren't always visibly in sight or consciously felt, especially amid unpleasant challenges, with an open heart, and a faithful mind. and a commitment to patience, I will come to know that peace and balance are on their way.

A Thought to Ponder at Dawn

Happiness and freedom are a direct reflection of my thoughts.

At every moment, while I'm thinking, I have a golden opportunity to show my strength by managing and policing my thoughts for my greater good.

My issues or concerns will find their resolution more quickly and easily when my mind considers choosing a new perspective and approach.

What challenges can I take on today by choosing a new approach just to confirm that this works?

A Thought to Ponder at Dusk

Taking a closer look to recognize that my identity is nothing more than a big, fabricated illusion that harbors my thoughts and feelings, can help exonerate *me - spirit -* from my captivating mind.

That realization gives my mind the ability to function in a more expanded manner, resulting in generating happier and healthier realities that can become a new standard.

A Thought to Ponder at Dawn

My mind can assess, evaluate, and judge, based on data collected by my brain.

The quality and efficiency level of this data is directly proportional to the accuracy and clarity of my mind's point of view. Although creating a clear and pure perception is not yet possible, I trust that my mind does its best with what it has to work with.

My inner wisdom says to trust my gut, which is another source of intelligence, while simultaneously being mindful of reality's imperfection. Things don't need to be perfect to have inner peace, calm, and balance.

A Thought to Ponder at Dusk

It may seem or even be impossible for me to stop my mind from judging people or things. By being aware that my mind judges, I can allow the thoughts to be as they are and accept them in the present moment.

The golden insight here is to allow and accept the fact that my mind is wired to judge and then not make any judgments anything more significant than they need to be. It's also possible for me to not give any greater credibility to my judgments as well.

When I realize that my judgments are made up and not true, I can begin accessing greater freedom for myself.

A Thought to Ponder at Dawn

Although my brain uses my body's sensory organs to collect data to assess my outside world, an enlightened mind is not tricked by the illusion of that which we call an *outside world*, and more readily turns inward for introspection and the creation of reality.

A Thought to Ponder at Dusk

An enlightened mind takes complete ownership of each interpretation that it makes and never points the finger at anything or anyone outside of itself for its creation.

To point the blame is to forfeit one's power and submit to being at the effect of others as well as circumstances.

A Thought to Ponder at Dawn

The power of my mind is strengthened when it learns to be responsible and accountable for everything that it creates especially when it knows that it's the creator.

More importantly, I hold no truth to any illusion that my mind creates especially since all reality is an illusion.

Realizing this, it would be in my best interests to take today and every day on like my life is like a Disney movie.

If by chance, I should find myself in a "Freddy Krueger" movie, there will be no one for me to point my finger at.

A Thought to Ponder at Dusk

An enlightened mind maintains its position in neutrality and doesn't need to seek alternatives or fix things.

This awareness creates a precious and endearing, non-reactive behavior. I reposition my mind by imagining a new reality that is non-reactive and allows my body to sense what that energetic shift feels like.

A Thought to Ponder at Dawn

When mindfulness exists within a community, there is a strong sense of belonging that is derived from selflessness in addition to a willful servitude towards others.

It's always refreshing to find like-minded souls who enjoy gathering for a good dose of nourishing familiarity.

Having good friend time is important to my health and well-being.

A Thought to Ponder at Dusk

Scientific discovery is what we base much of our reality around.

An authentic scientific approach to any particular focus of interest is to remain inside of the inquiry.

Once there is a particular discovery, it is human nature to get stuck inside the findings of what the inquiry process has provided, instead of remaining in the inquiry.

A Thought to Ponder at Dawn

Each now moment belongs neither to any past sums of infinite moments nor to any moments which have yet to appear in the infinite future.

Each now moment doesn't even belong to any mark of time… a moment, simply *is*.

Realizing this perspective during mediation brings a sense of freedom along with deep inner peace.

I intend to remain aware of particular moments throughout my day which seem special and apart from a moment that just passed.

A Thought to Ponder at Dusk

There is great joy in living a peaceful and balanced life which has resulted from surrendering to anything which I have no power over.

I surrender to the cycle of mother nature, to my belief in the Divine's order and plan, and to all of my fears, which are mostly about fearing fear itself.

A Thought to Ponder at Dawn

When I finally learned how to alter seasonal changes, control daily weather, extend the hours in a day, function effectively on little sleep, and figure out a way to live well into the hundreds, then I mastered the universe.

Until then, I remain blessed and privileged to be a part of the circle of life which I know little about. As I begin my day I will reflect on three things that I'm honestly grateful for.

A Thought to Ponder at Dusk

An Anytime Prayer for Anyone

God, Jesus, Mother Earth, Infinite Intelligence, and Saints of All Religions,

Help me to expand my heart and mind, deepen my intuition, and pay closer attention to my body's sensations as a way of directly communicating with me.

My heart and mind are grateful for my presence (*spirit*) and with devoted meditative practice, continue to deepen their faith in me.

As I create my sacred space within, I embrace all fears, be the love that I wish to see in the world and live freely inside of the Circle of Life.

A Thought to Ponder at Dawn

An awakened mind goes within to see what thoughts are being generated and observes without taking any responsive action.

Should there be any action to be taken, it would come as a result of inspiration for generating something new.

What can I generate today from my imagination that might inspire others?

A Thought to Ponder at Dusk

My mind's ability for self-reflection is an amazing gift.

It can help to shift my reality by relating more succinctly to whatever it perceives is going on outside.

A way to free me when I'm stuck with dysfunctional thoughts is to rethink what I choose to make real.

Remaining aware that all that is real, is valid and generated within my mind, ironically remains my sacred place of respite as well as my greatest creator of illusion.

A Thought to Ponder at Dawn

A process of creating a thought…

1. An experience occurs.
2. My brain collects whatever data it can.
3. My mind interprets limited data and uses past interpretations as its influential guide.
4. I add another point of view to my reality, which is mostly predicated on my past.

Understanding this process allows me to alter my interpretations, especially when they don't suit me, whenever I so choose.

A Thought to Ponder at Dusk

The grand scope of reality is a never-ending network of thoughts where everything is connected and related.

Ironically speaking, my reality is unique, just like everyone else's.

My mind also does its best to maintain a relatively strong and consistent thought pattern to satisfy having a subconscious fear-based need for stability.

My life will look unrecognizable when my mind is ready, has the courage, and allows itself to soar into uncharted territory.

A Thought to Ponder at Dawn

As the translator and reservoir of data and images, my mind continues to interpret and store information until it's needed to produce an outward projection using standard methods of communication. (let this sink in more deeply).

This strongly implies that whatever the experience is *out there*, its understanding is generated inside of my mind where it lives individually and is agreed upon collectively.

How can I take on my day with good intentions and be mindful that everything I think is really all made up?

A Thought to Ponder at Dusk

My reality is a culmination of both a finite network of existing thoughts and an infinite ocean of thoughts that have yet to be accessed.

My reality is only as flexible as my thoughts.

Rigidity is the cause of discomfort and dis-ease.

Exercising and stretching my thoughts by keeping my mind open allows a healthier flow of energy to maintain optimal mental health.

A Thought to Ponder at Dawn

With infinite potential and a strong will, I can enjoy an ever-changing and boundless assortment of realities.

When I uncover any dysfunctional beliefs still occupying my mind space, it's a great opportunity to create a happy replacement.

A Thought to Ponder at Dusk

I have considered my body to be like a machine when it comes time to maintain it.

I give it the needed nutritional energy and maintain it with exercise. My body, however, is not like a machine, but rather is an amazingly complex network of energy patterns that are generated from my thoughts.

Simply put, beautiful, nurturing, and harmonious thoughts radiate energetic vibrations for optimal health to thrive, while dysfunctional and sabotaging thoughts produce an array of dis-ease.

I am the chosen *Gate-Keeper* of the thoughts I wish to create and hold on to.

A Thought to Ponder at Dawn

An enlightened mind is blessed with so many things, one of which is to be freed from the blocks which have interrupted the beautiful steady streaming of thoughts that are mostly compassionate, kind, and loving.

Although this may not be a 24-hour occurrence just yet, mindfulness will help me to choose healthy beliefs over ones that might cause any dis-ease.

As I go through my day, I will take the time to check in to see how mindful I'm being.

A Thought to Ponder at Dusk

'I am that *I AM*' is a very old and profound statement, possibly requiring clarification.

When I am aware of myself as the *I AM*, without any thoughts to describe it, I recognize myself as solely a *being*.

This insight is only impactful for me when I realize how I can incorporate this into daily life.

At this time, I understand that I am that *I AM* is the closest I can get to the *truth*, and anything I place after the words, 'I AM'…, is contrived by me and those around me.

A Thought to Ponder at Dawn

Unconditional love and enlightenment are as much a part of reality's illusion as hate, greed, or any other negative illusion that I choose to make real.

The only difference is that the quality of life which I end up with is solely a byproduct of my interpretations.

I'm content when I can acknowledge being the source of this awesome illusion of human life.

A Thought to Ponder at Dusk

People often have something to say and yet conversations can sometimes get sticky when there are opposing views on a given subject.

Unpleasant arguments often result when we don't feel heard or respected for having our views.

How is it possible to introduce another vantage point without any upset?

The answer lies in being non-reactive and respectful while sharing, as well as being in agreement that multiple realities can exist at the same time, and usually do.

Day 348

A Thought to Ponder at Dawn

One path of least resistance is to listen to someone's perspective, gain an understanding of how they view their world and be considerate of that when relating to them from your perspective.

This is a bridge for harmony and fellowship and a notch up on communication skills.

A Thought to Ponder at Dusk

Regardless of how often I subconsciously reinforce that I'm not good enough, I'll never give up the notion that underneath it all, I also know that I'm special.

This is often a life-long battle between the subconscious and itself because of unsupervised guidance during childhood.

Every young mind creates a, 'not good enough' scenario at some point in childhood and never comes to realize that it was deeply mistaken and never *true*.

If this is still the case for me, I now have an opportunity to reprogram my old operating system with a new one of my own design.

A Thought to Ponder at Dawn

As a newly awakened individual, who still falls asleep now and then, I accept the challenge to practice being present and viewing reality with indifference and neutrality.

This is a cherished life-long commitment that will help me to access a mindset of possibility that I've never known and am excited to embrace.

A Thought to Ponder at Dusk

Creativity comes to me without any reason or evidence behind it because creation itself is completely generative.

Said differently, being creative is neither reasonable nor predictable.

What can I challenge myself to create at this moment that I didn't expect to even think about before reading this?

A Thought to Ponder at Dawn

I am the single *cause* who has my life looking like it does 'be-cause' I create and perpetuate a reality that is manifested through my interpretations.

No one does this for me, they're busy doing it for themselves. On one level of consciousness or another, I've agreed to everything that exists in my world.

This is the opportune access for me to be both responsible and accountable for the quality of my life.

A Thought to Ponder at Dusk

Approximately 2000 years ago, we first heard the expression, "We reap what we sow".

A cousin to this statement is, "Do unto others as you would have them do unto you". Just as every cause has an effect, the above statements are in alignment with karmic law.

The kicker, 'You can run, but you can't hide", allows me to realize the real playing field.

Realizing this may cause me to think twice before I speak because I'm the one responsible.

A Thought to Ponder at Dawn

Whatever my mind perceives and interprets creates a direct relationship to the quality of my existence.

Despite the thoughts which enter my mind, I am the "Gate-Keeper" who's responsible for which thoughts are voiced and which are left to disappear back to where they first originated.

Holding myself to account isn't always an easy task because it's too easy not to. However, when I'm mindful of the karmic boomerang effect which exists, it reminds me to stay on course and sharpen my moral skills as well as self-love. I will be mindful to witness what I'm thinking throughout today and see if I'm able to stop inappropriate thoughts from being spoken.

A Thought to Ponder at Dusk

Realize it or not, when I pay little attention to someone, it dismisses them from having their sense of significance and meaning in life.

This is a highly valuable insight to have around children as their minds are seeking to learn and communicate what they perceive and oftentimes seek confirmation or validation.

All children can use a little self-assurance now and then; this includes children of all ages.

A Thought to Ponder at Dawn

When I authentically listen to someone speak and am not just listening to respond, I gain a clearer and more genuine understanding of their vantage point.

Whether or not I agree or accept it for myself, is completely a different matter.

I don't have to agree with everything that others say or do, to have a close connection, when being respectful is the key component.

A Thought to Ponder at Dusk

My mind and body often take me on an energetic roller-coaster ride of past and future thoughts.

Despite always being in a stream of present moments, my mind usually doesn't focus on present moments because my reality's existence lives only inside of a remembered stream of passing moments.

When I'm in a meditative state, however, this is not the case because my focus is on my breath and the now.

A Thought to Ponder at Dawn

Although I can only exist in the moment, my mind notwithstanding has fooled itself into thinking otherwise.

A key to greater wisdom is realizing that every thought is an illusion, much of which is drawn on from long-gone interpretations.

Exploring how to take on my day while remaining awakened to the life maze of trick mirrors, can be a fun challenge if I reach out for assistance.

A Thought to Ponder at Dusk

There have been times when my intellectual mind believes that there's a much better place to be than where I am right now.

There is only one additional place, other than where I think that I am, that I can be and that's right here, right now, in the now moment.

Taking only a short three to five-minute break to focus on energetic intentions of peace and calm riding in and out on the carpet ride of my breath, allows me to gain my power center rather quickly.

A Thought to Ponder at Dawn

A healthy mind might have a surmountable challenge when discerning between fabricated realities and fictive truths.

An enlightened mind knows no difference.

Today I realize that both an autobiography and a biography are the same as a novel. Although there is factual content, significance, and validity to the stories, all of reality is an illusion.

A Thought to Ponder at Dusk

Many inherited beliefs powerfully suggest that no matter what, we will never be good enough or happy, causing us to seek out ways to feel better, hence, the self-help industry.

This is a universal challenge for all people and is strangely comforting to know that no one is alone with this crazy flaw in our mind's design. Knowing that the belief of not being good enough isn't really *true*, still doesn't allow for transformation to occur because the mind wants to fix everything immediately.

Transformation requires being aware to witness the mind's willingness to first allow and accept the current challenge and be with it before any shifts can occur; simple, not easy.

Day 355

A Thought to Ponder at Dawn

The process of transformation always occurs in the present moment.

Anytime there's an upset of any magnitude, redirecting my focus on my breath right now, allows me to return to calm, peace, and love, fairly quickly and without a need to fix it.

A key part of any transformation is creating a shift in perspective for the challenge at hand.

Realizing that infinitesimal realities exist, I can freely choose one that empowers me.

A Thought to Ponder at Dusk

Honoring my word is a source of my integrity and with integrity, comes power. My words can help to raise and empower a person or tear them down pretty quickly. Reminding others of the powerful and significant impact that their words have helps them feel empowered and inspired to make a difference for others.

Words are real, valid, significant, and packed with meaning and energetic intention. No matter how wonderful or grave a situation may be, I always have the option to choose words that are kind, caring, compassionate, and understanding, to move the conversation in a positive direction. When I reflect on my day and recall the words I've spoken, I am grateful to see where I can do a better job tomorrow.

A Thought to Ponder at Dawn

Removing myself daily from everyday life and going to a space where I can quiet my mind and listen carefully to what my body is trying to tell me, allows me to reset, rejuvenate and revive both my mind and body.

In only 30-60 minutes of focused intention, this beautiful reset happens. This is a daily, *to me – from me* gift, it costs nothing and yields wonderful results.

A Thought to Ponder at Dusk

Although having a collective agreement doesn't make anything *truer*, it certainly reinforces and confirms which thoughts will continue to be held as real by the majority.

For example, when everyone believed that the world was flat, it didn't matter if the minority didn't agree because it wasn't proven.

Even after it was fact, people still related to a flat world as *true* for quite some time.

The strong resistance to making something *untrue* often short-circuits the mind.

Day 357

A Thought to Ponder at Dawn

When I have an experience, I make the gross mistake to say, 'My experience is…". This is not the case because although I did have an experience, 'My interpretation of the experience is…", is much more accurate and empowering communication.

For example, five people are watching a movie and have the same experience, and yet they have five different interpretations of the same experience.

Countless examples are everywhere - in sports, government, relationships, religious beliefs, etc.; as long as we have an individual mind, it produces its own perspective.

The important thing for me to remember is that while I only have my interpretation of an experience and not the experience itself, I must never forget that what I perceived is never *true*.

A Thought to Ponder at Dusk

Being in a state of thoughtlessness is an experience and cannot be understood with 100% accuracy.

In addition, being in any experience is always interpreted after it occurs, confirming that an experience is personal and without words.

A Thought to Ponder at Dawn

All that exists is now and wherever I place my focus in any given moment, challenges my mind to remain aware of living inside the streaming of now moments.

As I ready myself for today, this now moment is, was, and will always be, all there is. I rarely realize that there is nowhere to go, nothing to do, and nothing to get, while I am right here, right now.

How this plays out throughout my day is to realize this whenever I find myself stuck or challenged with anything, for it too shall pass as quickly as favorable moments. Going with the flow of my day is something that requires being aware of as it happens.

A Thought to Ponder at Dusk

It would be wise for me to make a habit to perform a continuous *reality check* on myself to recognize the extent to which I love and like myself. Since I'm the only one who gets to be with me 100% of the time, wherever I go and whatever I do, it might be a great idea to be in a state of love with who and what I am.

Loving myself is allowing and accepting everything that I am and everything that I'm not. Any lingering attachment to a personal regret is the telltale sign of transformation yet to occur and a reminder for me to remain in gratitude for all that is good.

A Thought to Ponder at Dawn

An open mind is an expanding mind. Expanding minds live in life's wonder, fun exploration, welcome research, and place less focus on the results because most things are yesterday's news anyway.

What would today look like for me if I approached it like there was never a day on the planet thus far, like it? To see the same old things that I come to know daily with a sense of newness as I've never seen them before, would allow access to a much greater and more advanced perspective, one which has little if any history. I welcome the challenge and accept the newness as I've never done before.

A Thought to Ponder at Dusk

Since birthdays are very real and yet not *true*, what can I say about how old I am and what my life expectancy will be?

Can I start walking around sayin' that I'm 17,155 days on the planet if I just turned 47? Can I also say that I'm 564 months old today at 47? Shall I be bold enough to shout out that I'm 411,720 hours old now that I'm 47?

Question: If all of the data here is correct, why then is 47 the only correct answer? Answer: Collective Agreement. Not configuring 47 years in 'seconds' saves many pages and a lot of writing.

A Thought to Ponder at Dawn

I have the potential to enjoy limitless and ever-changing realities and also have the free will needed to make them manifest.

What's in my reality wallet that I'd like to take on today?

Thinking of today's schedule, what perspectives might I want to alter so that my day is rich, and fulfilling, and leaves me fully empowered?

A Thought to Ponder at Dusk

Reality shifts effortlessly when my mind flows with its own creations.

The degree of mindfulness while creating my day determines the impact that I will have on people and things around me.

At night, I can put my daytime persona away and delve into a world of restful sleep. Many important things occur in sleep and yet are without my knowledge.

The practice of remaining conscious while in a dream state is possible although it's not a world I've yet to fully understand.

A Thought to Ponder at Dawn

An enlightened mind is blessed to have relinquished many of the blocks which interrupt or infringe upon the streaming flow of thoughts.

The happy Buddha represents the freedom and exhilaration which is felt from living inside of expanded consciousness and recognizes the silliness of whatever illusions would normally cause the mind any discomfort.

Today I will be a happy Buddha and no matter what challenges may occur, I will remain light-hearted.

A Thought to Ponder at Dusk

When I allow myself to be as I am, wherever I am, and accept a situation for being as it is without seeking to alter anything, I am practicing mindfulness.

When I have insomnia, for example, I will allow and accept it to be just as it is.

I then can take my meditation beads and redirect my focus onto thoughts that bring peace and calm, leaving insomnia to exist as it is. Before I know it, I find myself waking up to begin a new day.

A Thought to Ponder at Dawn

My mind knows calm, peace, and joy when the undercurrent of having to fix anything becomes silent.

Although this may sound silly, *having* to be in action is not the same as being in action without having to do so, mainly because the dis-ease of a dysfunctional motivator is absent.

Removing any unhealthy impetus allows me to act with freedom and inspiration.

A Thought to Ponder at Dusk

A soul-conscious mind often ministers to others with unconditional love and doesn't get distracted by the illusion of mending something which has never needed mending.

In quiet and stillness, I delve deeper into my mind and awaken my subconscious by reinforcing the goodness of my intentions.

A Thought to Ponder at Dawn

Choosing unconditional love, kindness, and creating a path toward enlightenment, are as much a part of life's illusions as choosing to hate and be greedy.

Whatever I acknowledge as real and however I choose to live, provides the quality of life that I lead...and as I reap, so shall I sow.

A Thought to Ponder at Dusk

As I awaken to creating a path towards enlightenment, I promise myself to be open to all that is possible, no matter what.

Repeating this slowly and like I've never said it before, creates another vantage point, from which new thoughts become possible.

I welcome newness and wonder in every moment.

A Thought to Ponder at Dawn

Without my mind's ability to interpret and create life's illusions, life would be void of any meaning and I'd be bored as heck.

I understand that my life is simply just my life and yet the gift that our species brings to the table is a rainbow of colorful interpretations which are limitless.

A Thought to Ponder at Dusk

One great path of least resistance is to listen and observe someone's perspective, gain an honest understanding of how they view their world and take that fully into consideration when relating to them.

This behavior increases the possibility for them to be open to hearing another perspective, mine perhaps.

This behavior offers a pretty reliable outcome every time because all we want is to be heard and understood.

Day 365

A Thought to Ponder at Dawn

Today I will test out a different way of communicating: I'll pretend that no one wants to hear what I have to say and that everyone just wants to share about themselves.

I will wear a ring, a bracelet, or even a watch, which I've not worn in a while, as a secret reminder for me to ask open-ended questions to people and then closely listen to them. Should they ask about me, I'll answer and quickly turn the conversation back onto them. My main intention is to fully understand them and learn how they think.

This dynamic is not the standard way for me, I'll be mindful not to listen to respond, but rather to listen so that I can fully understand. In the evening when I remove my secret reminder, reflecting on the day will let me know how successful I was in getting to know people. When done properly, I may choose to continue this behavior and see where it takes me.

A Thought to Ponder at Dusk

I take this moment and think of one of the coolest things that I'd like to see happen. I'll close my eyes and imagine that it has already happened. I'll remain in this reality shift for 15 - 20 minutes and allow myself to refocus on those thoughts energetically permeating every cell in my body. Continuing this practice may open my consciousness to a world I've not experienced before.

About the Author

Brooklyn born and raised, this fat, ugly, and stupid kid, who also thought he had issues with his sexual identity from the age of five, while not knowing what that even meant at the time, finally awakened at the ripe old age of 47 to learn that not one bit of it was true.

My awakened life began anew at 47, and although it didn't remove any part of my past, with proper guidance, it was put in its place with proper perspective. Hopefully, this book will help to do the same for you should that remain incomplete.

As a young child, I remember always feeling special and always wanting to hug everyone because I knew how it made everyone feel. Yet, from zero to 12 (the impressionable years), many significant things in my life showed up to be quite unpleasant. I sadly remember many days of wishing I was dead. At 12 years old, with the onset of hormones and an astute mother who saw that her kid was in trouble, she took on a second job to send me to the sleep-away camp of my dreams - Rawhide Ranch, where I would live out my childhood dream of being a cowboy... and I did.

This is where I and my childhood family of friends blossomed. I became a rancher, a junior wrangler, an assistant wrangler, and finally a wrangler, who headed up the Broncos, a group of 13 and 14-year-old boys whom I taught to horseback ride. Little did I know that the span of years from 13 to 26 would also be the impetus for whatever success came my way.

Growing up with a reading comprehension problem from first grade, being made fun of because I was fat, and being bullied with name-calling like ugly thrown into the mix, I became quite the introvert and mama's boy. This was a reality that I conjured up in my own mind and didn't have the wherewithal to ever realize that none of it was true. Yet, having circumstances like that occur for any of us, shapes, and sentences many of us for the rest of our lives. So, here's this kid who thinks that he's stupid and goes off and graduates high school in three years instead of four with honors and graduates college in four years instead of five, with a double major in biology and psychology. By graduation, I was only 21 and still had 26 years more to go to open my eyes. However, my teenage years began to help alter my views of being ugly because that was the onset of dating season.

Onto life after college. I fell in love with a beautiful blonde-haired, blue-eyed woman from another state that I met at a party. Then, my life took a sharp turn away from my interest in becoming a large animal Veterinarian specializing in horses. The other option to consider was to become a Clinical Psychologist to help bring awareness to the short-circuiting that occurred in my childhood's interpretations from needlessly occurring to other kids.

Instead, I moved out of state, jobless and without a form of transportation, and lived with my future ex-wife (get that?)

Initially, I took on a job as a pet store manager and found that I loved hand-taming the birds and dealing with customers. Unfortunately, it was a family business, and they eventually decided to close within the year from hiring me.

My first significant job was in sales at a mid-sized company. To no one's surprise but my own, I made sales rookie of the year and won a trip to Hawaii. I told my wife I wasn't happy with what I was doing. Although I had learned quite well how to sell a torch at a corner fire, I felt empty inside because it lacked integrity, and I didn't like that behavior, so I forfeited my trip to Maui and quit after creating a new plan and direction.

I challenged myself to think about what else I could do and take it on without quitting. The only thing that came to mind was cutting hair. As far back as Rawhide Ranch, I've always cut hair throughout my college years. In college, I paid for my books and had extra spending money as well. It was set. I went to beauty college, and during my time there, the school hired an international award-winning professional to train me for the International Beauty Competition in New York City. Although my career as a Hair Designer had an incredible launch after taking home a trophy for my school, I learned early on that hairdressers didn't quite have the standing they deserved in the professional world. It was now my job to alter that, and so I did.

I became a Director of Education for a hair color company headquartered in Paris, France, wrote their encyclopedia on hair color theory, studied extensively through Europe, and then toured throughout the United States to teach the staff who would train my constituents throughout the US. (Keep in mind, I'm still not 47 yet.)

When the timing was right, I stepped away from that role and decided to earn my fair share of varicose veins by standing behind a chair for the next few decades. I opened a Day Spa salon when day spas were popping up. Looking back, being a serial entrepreneur and working in the world of Hair Design has allowed me to touch the hearts and minds of countless people, many of whom remain a lifelong family of friends.

Finally, the impetus for why this book has made it into your hands was due to a three to six-month-to-live diagnosis from having a very rare form of head and neck cancer at the ripe age, you guessed it, 47.

Often, it takes either a life-threatening challenge or something significant to cause us to pause from our daily repetitious routines to awaken the human mind. My diagnosis did just that.

With as much kindness as I can muster, I will share that head and neck radiation therapy is, at best, the most brutal treatment you can give to a living being. Enough said.

The only saving grace was to have had a near-death experience, which shifted my perspective into a realm I never thought possible.

I became a minister and have been in service for 18 years as a Transformational Reality Coach.

Peace, Joy, and Laughter to you today and always.

Hugs to your heart,

Ron Baron

www.ingramcontent.com/pod-product-compliance
Lightning Source LLC
Chambersburg PA
CBHW052028090426

42739CB00010B/1826